The Man Who Touched the Sky

ALSO BY JOHNNY ACTON

Soup

Mushroom

JOHNNY ACTON

The Man Who Touched the Sky

Hodder & Stoughton

First published in Great Britain in 2002 by Hodder and Stoughton
A division of Hodder Headline

1 3 5 7 9 10 8 6 4 2

A CIP catalogue record for this title is
available from the British Library

ISBN 0 340 81932 4

Typeset in Sabon by Palimpsest Book Production Limited,
Polmont, Stirlingshire
Printed and bound in Great Britain by
Clays Ltd, St Ives plc

Hodder and Stoughton
A division of Hodder Headline
338 Euston Road
London NW1 3BH

To Percy, with all my love

CONTENTS

ILLUSTRATIONS

Piccard cuts a celebratory cake modelled on his balloon *FNRS*
Explorer II prior to its launch from the Stratobowl in South Dakota, 1935

Page 7   A fully kitted-up Joe Kittinger prepares to depart the Earth in *Excelsior III*, 1960
Excelsior III photographed at 40,000 feet

Page 8   Kittinger steps out into the void, 102,800 feet above New Mexico

Picture Acknowledgements

© Betmann/CORBIS: 4 above right, 6 above left. © CORBIS: 6 below. © Hulton Archive/Getty Images: 2 below, 3 below, 5 above. © Hulton-Deutsch Collection/CORBIS: 6 above right. Private Collection: 1, 2 above, 3 above, 4 above left and below. © US Air Force/National Geographic Society, Image Collection: 7 below. © Volkmar Wentzel/National Geographic Society, Image Collection: 7 above, 8.

ACKNOWLEDGEMENTS

I have many people to thank for enabling me to write this book: my wife, father, in-laws and other relatives, who together with my long-suffering friends, have all endured more conversation about balloons than they can ever have bargained for; Duke Gildenberg, for a fascinating morning in a hotel lobby in Alamogordo; Ruth Rendell, for her sage advice; Dave Goldblatt and Simon Aylwin, for hours of stimulating discussion about the meaning of the sky; Pippa Dennis, for her contacts list; Julia Barder, for her unsolicited and very welcome PR job; Paul Moss, for patiently explaining to me why airborne balloons move along with the Earth as it rotates (it's because of inertia); and the many others who have inspired and encouraged me, or furnished me with vital information along the way. On the professional front, I have been lucky enough to have a truly talented team behind me: Jonny Geller, my agent, whose words were the initial catalyst for the book ('write about something uplifting'), and who took about five seconds to come up with the title; his assistant Doug Kean; Roland Philipps, Lizzie Dipple and Juliet Brightmore at Hodder, who have all been great to work with; and Hazel Orme for her wonderful copy-editing.

AUTHOR'S NOTE ON TEMPERATURES AND DISTANCES

This is a vexed issue for reasons geographical, historical, and generational. In the end, I have elected to express temperatures in terms of both Fahrenheit and Celsius, largely because this is what British readers have become accustomed to through television weather forecasts. Distances, on the whole, I have chosen to express in imperial units. There are two main reasons for this: first, this is in keeping with usual practice in the majority of places and eras featured in the book; second, 100,000 feet is a key figure in the story that follows, and I simply find it more satisfactory as an expression of a 'landmark' than the metric alternative, which is 30,480 metres. On a very few occasions I have gone metric out of submission to convention (for example, in discussing the wavelengths of ultraviolet light).

For the record, one metre is equal to 3.2808 feet, hence 10,000 metres is 32,808 feet. One mile, meanwhile, is 5,280 feet, or 1609.34 metres. Joe Kittinger's peak altitude during the Excelsior project may therefore be variously expressed as 102,800 feet, 31,333.4 metres, or 19.47 miles.

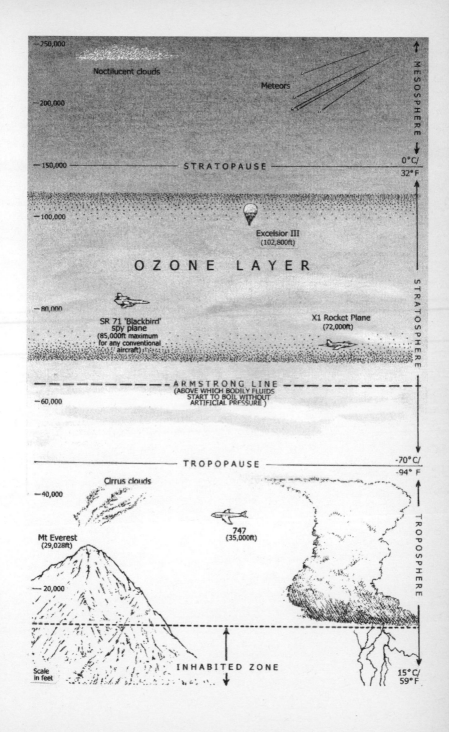

PROLOGUE

On 16 August 1960, Joe Kittinger went up in a balloon. He kept going up. And then he went up some more. It was only when he had risen beyond the very borders of space, to a height of 102,800 feet, that *Excelsior III* silently shimmered to a halt.

He found himself in a paradoxical world of preternatural colour where the Sun blazed from a sky as black as pitch. Below him, the curve of the Earth was plainly visible. Individual clouds were now so tiny that they were more about texture than shape. And all that separated him from an instant, messy death was the thin skin of his standard-issue US Air Force partial-pressure suit.

For as long as there had been people to dream, they had dreamed of going beyond the edge of the sky. The same ambition had burned in every child who ever climbed a tree. Now, at long last, someone had made it.

What Kittinger saw beneath him would change our view of ourselves and our world for ever. Above him beckoned a vast, virgin arena for human exploration. In less than nine years, men would plant their feet on their first extraterrestrial heavenly body. But at that moment, Joe Kittinger was in much the same position as the first lungfish who risked slithering out of the sea on to the beach.

Just like that lungfish, Kittinger didn't hang around to savour the experience. He took one long last look at the extraordinary panorama laid out before him, said a quick prayer, and threw himself into the void.

Chapter One

THE DREAM

Now the whole earth had one language and few words. And as men migrated from the east, they found a plain in the land of Shinar and settled there. And they said to one another, 'Come, let us build ourselves a city, and a tower with its top in the heavens, and let us make a name for ourselves . . .'

And the Lord came down to see the city and the tower, which the sons of men had built. And the Lord said, 'Behold, they are one people and they have all one language, and this is only the beginning of what they will do, and nothing that they propose to do will now be impossible for them. Come, let us go down and there confuse their language, that they may not understand one another's speech.'

So the Lord scattered them abroad over the face of all the earth, and they left off building the city.

(Genesis 11:1–8)

To our distant ancestors, the sky was a place of unspeakable wonder. Ever-changing yet immutable, always present but perpetually out of reach, it could only be the realm of the gods. It was certainly home to godlike beings, like the free-floating clouds and the great arching discs that lit the world day and night, which were somehow exempt from the laws that bound everything earthly.

If the sheer otherness of the sky suggested its divinity, its determining influence on human affairs seemed to confirm it. After all, the sky and its objects dictated, in the most literal sense, what went on beneath them.

Sometimes this influence was felt directly, as when the clouds chose to release or withhold their life-giving rain, or the Sun its warmth. At other times, the sky worked more obliquely, sending messages that depended on human interpretation for their full realisation. The stars in particular offered cues and omens for the guidance of those who knew how to read them. The clouds, too, bore messages, both prosaically, in terms of what they presaged about the weather, and poetically, by inspiring the scriveners who used them for divination.

The sky's mystery was compounded by its extraordinary dual nature. By day, it was fluid and ever-changing, as the clouds went about their unfathomable life-cycles. But at night, in the mesmerising stillness of its stars, it was all about eternity.

This juxtaposition of regular and 'chaotic' elements in the sky had a crucial role in the birth of the notion of time. Time requires not only a flow of events but also a predictable and reliable pattern against which to measure it. Only in the sky were such patterns available. Some early civilisations used the gap between two new moons as their yardstick, others the period between days when the Sun rose at exactly the same point on the horizon. But, like everything else in Nature, all of them oriented themselves by the movements of the heavens. When it came to deciding when to plant seed or move flocks, people turned to the great clock of the sky.

If the foregoing were not enough, the sky was also fantastically beautiful. Looked at coldly, this was perhaps to be expected: from an evolutionary point of view, harmony with the environment is crucial, and it would have been highly perverse of Nature not to have equipped her creatures with an instinctual liking for the ceiling under which they were inevitably going to live. What we can say is that if this was her motive, she certainly made an excellent job of it. Even today, few things move us so deeply as the sky, from the pristine, icy beauty of a starry night to the exuberant warmth of dawn and sunset. At such times, the sky is the very essence of poetry.

But if the sky could be hypnotically lovely, it could also be terrifying. Thunder and lightning were impossibly awesome to our forebears. When we consider how these phenomena retain the power to humble us, in spite of all our insights into how they are generated, we can gain some idea of the impression they must have made. Many cultures attributed thunder and lightning to the wrath of powerful deities. The Ancient Greeks believed they were the weapons of Zeus, while the Vikings thought they were forged in the workshop of the god Thor. Some societies even recognised the sky as their supreme being: the Babylonians wrote the name of their chief god Anu with the identical sign they used for the heavens. Most located their gods in the sky.

The Ancient Chinese encapsulated the sky's strange complementary otherness in a belief that it was circular while the Earth was square. In a world filled with magic, the sky was in an altogether different league. To many, it must have seemed the very face of God. But it was also impossibly remote. Or was it just tantalisingly out of reach?

Of earthly creatures, only the mysterious birds had a foot in both camps. As a consequence, their feathers were often revered as semi-divine. Angels, the intermediaries between gods and men, were also portrayed with wings. What could it be like up there, in the realm where such beings were free to fly? Man stared up at the sky in wonder. For now, that was all he could do.

———

According to traditional Maori mythology, the Earth and the sky were not always separate as they are today. In the beginning, they were locked together in a perpetual act of copulation. But although they conceived many times in this manner, their embrace was so tight that their children were denied room in which to grow. The union put the birth of the world on hold.

Stifling in their dark constriction, the children of Ranginui, the sky god, and his consort Papatuanuuku debated murdering their parents as a way out of their predicament. Alone of his siblings, Tane, the forest spirit, demurred. With all his might, he pushed his head against his father and his feet against his mother until he had wrenched them apart.

Of all the children of Papatuanuuku and Ranginui, only Uru, the god of the air, elected to stay with his father. But he was so silent that Ranginui eventually forgot he was there. In his loneliness, Uru wept, his tears freezing to become the stars. Meanwhile, the bereft sky god, condemned to gaze down at his beautiful lost wife for ever, had tears of his own to weep. They fell, and continue to fall, as rain.

Many cultures tell similar stories of a primordial separation between the Earth and the sky. Typically, the Big Split is preceded by a golden age in which the two worlds are connected. While this harmony reigns, people and spirits move freely between the realms, and death is as yet unknown. Then disaster strikes. Somehow, the link is severed. From now on, man is confined to the Earth.

Some societies blame the gods for this cosmic rupture. In parts of Ghana, the chief deity is said to have pulled the sky away from the Earth because the women kept striking it with their pounding sticks while they were grinding meal. Essentially, he did it because he had a headache. Other peoples attribute the rift to events that are, in the deepest of senses, absurd. The Nuer of southern Sudan, for example, believe that a hungry hyena gnawed through the rope that once connected Earth with the heavens. Thus the human predicament is effectively boiled down to Murphy's Law. If it can go wrong, it will.

A third tendency, and perhaps the most common, is to place the responsibility squarely on the shoulders of mankind. In this version of events, the separation of Earth and sky is the direct result of human disobedience, like the biblical expulsion from the Garden of Eden.

Doubtless we can learn a great deal about a society and its levels of existential guilt from a study of which, if any, of these three mechanisms it invokes to explain the gulf between the world and the heavens. But the similarities between these stories are even more striking than their differences. Some psychologists have hypothesised that they have their origins in the universal but 'forgotten' experience of birth. The parallels are certainly striking, not least in the recurring motif of a connecting rope, tree or ladder, which is subsequently severed and removed. And in both scenarios perfect, weightless union is followed by the crushing and isolating experience of gravity.

There is another sense, too, in which myths of the separation of Earth and sky might be said to echo our births. Perhaps in both cases, at some level, we never quite let go of the dream that the process might be reversed . . .

Lest we be tempted to dismiss such stories as the cute artefacts of 'primitive' societies, we should remind ourselves that a similar legend plays an important role in the first few chapters of the book of Genesis. And whatever we make of those ancient biblical tales, it is difficult to deny that they are expressions, however 'poetic', of some of humanity's deepest and earliest-held beliefs.

At one level, the story of the Tower of Babel, with which this chapter begins, appears to be a myth to account for the existence of ziggurats – mysterious towers, dotted about the deserts of Mesopotamia, which were already old at the time of the composition of the Bible. At another, related level, the story is evidently a dig at the then Middle Eastern superpower of Babylon, whose expansionist policies represented a serious threat to the religion of the Israelites. The Hebrew word for Babylon is identical to the one used for the city with the tower, and it was well known that in the centre of her capital there stood an enormous seven-tiered ziggurat, Etementaki, the House of the Foundation of Heaven and Earth. But behind this political slant, yet another tradition is discernible, this one more ancient than the rest. The inference to be drawn from Yahweh's sabotage of the Babel building project is clear: the sky is forbidden territory, and any attempt to breach it will be strenuously resisted.

———

The clouds and Sun and Moon and stars were a ceaseless reminder to early man that he was fallen and lived in a fallen world, falling being exactly what the sky and its objects did not do. It was inevitable, however, that over the years some people would try to overturn the apparent order of things and take to the air. Equally inevitably, the majority wound up with broken necks.

To emphasise the need for humans to keep to their place, the Ancient Greeks told themselves a story. Its main protagonist was a young man named Icarus. He was the son of Daedalus, an ingenious Athenian artisan who had murdered his nephew Talus in a fit of professional jealousy after the latter had invented the saw. For this crime, Daedalus was exiled to the island of Crete, where he was placed in the service of King Minos. At the time, Crete was being terrorised by the Minotaur, the monstrous love-child of Minos' wife Pasiphae and a bull given to the king by the sea god Poseidon. Daedalus was immediately given the task of constructing a prison to contain the fearsome beast. The result was the celebrated

Labyrinth, where the Minotaur was kept sated on human flesh, exacted as tribute from Athens.

Eventually, the Athenian king Theseus decided to try to end this drain on his human resources. With the help of Minos' daughter Ariadne, Theseus extracted the secret of the Labyrinth from Daedalus. With this information, he was able to find and slay the Minotaur and subsequently to return to Athens.

When Minos discovered what had happened, he had Daedalus and his young son Icarus thrown into the Labyrinth. But Daedalus, who had lost none of his ingenuity, vowed to find a way for the pair to escape. He hatched a plan whereby he and Icarus would attempt to fly to Sicily, using wings he constructed from feathers and wax. As he strapped the smaller pair on to his son, he warned him of the perils of trying to fly too high during the journey. But Icarus, intoxicated by the thrill of flying, ignored him. He climbed too close to the Sun, and the wax that held his wings together melted. Icarus hurtled into the sea and was killed.

At first glance, the myth of Icarus appeared to set the seal on man's predicament. He longed to travel up to the sky, but it seemed to have been placed for ever beyond his reach. It was dangerous and possibly impious even to try. But diehard dreamers who read the small print noticed that in all the excitement over Icarus' demise something significant had been overlooked: old man Daedalus had arrived safely in Sicily. The hope remained that one day, somehow, the Earth and the heavens would be reunited.

Chapter Two

FIRST ATTEMPTS

In 1785, just two years after man had finally cracked the age-old riddle of flight, the Anglo-Italian scientist and historian Tiberius Cavallo wrote these wise words: 'The tales of antiquity, the poetical productions, the religious tenets, and even the histories, of most nations, shew that to acquire the art of flying, or of imitating the birds, has been the earnest desire, and has exercised the genius, of mankind in every age.' There was, however, an important caveat to be attached to old accounts of attempts at flying: 'With some, it is a question whether those allegorical passages are merely the produce of the imagination, ever fond of raising itself into the pure and unencumbered regions above the surface of the Earth . . .'

Some of the earliest tales of human flight certainly seem more motivated by a desire to boost the reputations of their subjects than by scrupulous dedication to reality. A case in point is the legendary account of Alexander the Great getting off the ground by tying to his throne some griffons, which he is then supposed to have cajoled into flying upwards by waving hunks of meat skewered on his sword above their noses. To get back down, so goes the story, he simply dangled the bait beneath them.

The first people we can be reasonably sure succeeded in leaving the ground for any length of time did so for spiritual reasons. From the earliest times religious seekers had climbed mountains to escape worldly concerns and commune with the divine. Many cultures found it natural to house their gods in the mountains, at the top of the peak they believed to be the highest in the world. From such a vantage-point, the deities could expect an uninterrupted view of the entire planet. In the case of the Ancient Greeks, the divine mountain was Olympus, at 9520 feet.

This association between divinity and altitude crops up everywhere. The prophets of the Old Testament waged a constant battle against the rival Canaanite religion with its seductive regard for the 'high places'. Moses went up Mount Sinai and returned with the Ten Commandments. The Tibetan Buddhists secreted their monasteries high among the peaks of the Himalayas. Some individuals simply took things a step further by constructing their own route up into the heavens.

It must be admitted at the outset that, from a strictly technical point of view, these pioneers were cheating – they could never completely relinquish some sort of physical connection to the Earth. But their achievements marked them out as unusually brave individuals, which they had to be if they were going to risk sticking their heads into the realm of the divine. Their experiences also provided a foretaste of the psychological challenges man would have to face on his way upwards.

An early account of this kind of spiritual practice was written by Lucian of Samosata in the middle of the second century. In *De Syria Dea*, he described how there stood in the gateway of the temple of Atoragatis in the city of Hierapolis two enormous towers, or 'phalli' (which he claimed, a touch hyperbolically, were about 1800 feet high). Twice a year, he went on, 'A man climbs up on one of these phalli and lives in the tip for a period of seven days. This reason is given for the ascent: the populace believes that he communes with the gods on high and asks for blessings on all Syria, and that the gods hear his prayers from nearby.'

A similar desire to get nearer to the divine seems to have underpinned the bizarre but well-documented behaviour of the great Simeon Stylites, who lived from 390 to 459 AD. A century after his death, the historian Evagrius neatly summarised what it appeared he was up to: 'In these times flourished and became illustrious Simeon, of holy and famous memory, who originated the contrivance of stationing himself on top of a column . . . This man, endeavouring to realise in the flesh the existence of the heavenly hosts, lifts himself above the concerns of Earth, and overpowering the downward tendency of man's nature, is intent on things above.' For almost half a century, this hardcore ascetic lived up a series of increasingly lofty poles. Sometimes, to compound the self-mortification, he would remain standing for weeks on end on the tiny platform at the summit, like a living Nelson atop his column. Today, we would probably lock him up. The only debate would be whether the experience drove him mad, or whether he was crazy to begin with. To his contemporaries, though, Simeon was the most venerable figure imaginable. He was literally closer to God than everyone else. As a result, people flocked to him from all over the ancient world, seeking his advice and asking him to intercede for them.

If even the exalted Simeon needed a prop, the early Christians were never likely to be receptive to claims of unsupported flight. But the rumours refused to die away completely. Bishop Agobard of Lyons, who died in 840, was roused to fury by the naïvety of some of his parishioners. 'We have seen and heard,' he wrote, 'of many people overcome with so much foolishness, made crazy by so much stupidity, that they believe and say that there is a certain region, which is called Magonia, from which ships come in the clouds. In these ships, the crops that fell because of hail and were lost in storms are carried back into that region; evidently these aerial sailors make a payment to the storm-makers, and take the grain and other crops.' Agobard even had to preside over (and summarily dismiss) a trial of three men and a woman brought to him by locals who insisted they had fallen from such ships and deserved to be stoned for their banditry. There is no clue in this account as to how the Magonians were supposed to have achieved their feat.

The same could be said of the anonymous hero of an enigmatic item that appeared in a London newsletter in September 1607: 'The greatest newes in this countrie is of an ingenious fellow, that in Barkeshire sailed or went over a high steeple in a boat, all of his own making; and without any other help than himself in her, conveyed her above twenty miles by land over hills and dales and so to London.' Tiberius Cavallo was no doubt correct to put down such tales to wishful thinking. What really tells against them, however, is that the technologies they presumably relied on never caught on. When a viable means of flying was discovered, its usage spread like wildfire.

The one group who had a measure of success were the tower-jumpers. In 1010, a monk named Elimer, inspired by the gliding of jackdaws, attached artificial wings to his limbs and leaped from the roof of the abbey church in Malmesbury, Wiltshire. He flew a few hundred feet before he panicked and plunged to the ground, breaking both his legs. In the 1630s Hezarfen Ahmet Celebi put on a rather better performance. He donned a pair of rushwork wings, jumped off the Galata tower in Istanbul and flew right across the Bosphorus to the Asian side of the city. At first, he was much fêted by the then sultan, Murat IV. Eventually, however, the sultan grew paranoid in the proximity of such a genius. 'This man is to be feared,' he is quoted as saying. 'He can do anything he wishes. The presence of such men is not auspicious.' Accordingly, Celebi was exiled to Algeria, where he died in obscurity.

As impressive as these aerial adventures were, they were demonstrations of gliding rather than of true flying. The fact is that until the late eighteenth century, man drew a blank in terms of getting himself off the ground, at least for more than a few hair-raising seconds.*

There are, however, some tantalising accounts of people persuading inanimate objects to fly. The Chinese were precocious in this arena. *The Ten Thousand Infallible Arts of the Prince of Huai-Nan*, written in the second century BC, claims that 'eggs can be made to fly in the air by the aid of burning tinder' (an ancient commentary on this text explains that this can be done by stuffing a little piece of burning mugwort inside an evacuated egg). The principle may well have been suggested by the first paper lanterns, which were developed during this period. It can only have been a matter of time before one of these lightweight globes, perhaps one with an exceptionally small upper opening, was placed over a vigorous flame and tried to take off of its own accord. Certainly, the Chinese have been making paper balloons for centuries. Nevertheless, the idea of building one large enough to carry a man skywards appears to have eluded them.

Back in Europe, Archytas of Taranto in Sicily was supposed to have invented a wooden pigeon capable of flight in about the year 4 BC. A contemporary historian ventured the theory that this bird was 'suspended by balancing, and was animated by an occult and enclosed aura of spirit', but he was unable to be more precise. Meanwhile the German magician John Muller (a.k.a. Regiomontanus), who died in 1436, was said

---

* One possible exception was flagged up in 1974, when Jim Woodman and Julian Nott showed that it was at least *possible* that the ancient inhabitants of Nazca in Peru had built balloon-like devices. Using a similar logic to that invoked by Thor Heyerdahl during the *Kon Tiki* expedition, Nott and Woodman constructed a balloon using materials and technology that would have been available to the Peruvian locals fifteen hundred years before (indeed, they employed the same craftsman who had built Heyerdahl's raft). The smoke-filled, reed-and-cotton *Condor I* carried both men to a height of 300 feet.

to have built an iron fly that could fly around the room and back to his hand.

In both instances, it is not impossible that the inventors were on to something – Cavallo, for instance, believed that Regiomontanus did it with magnetism – but chose to keep the secrets to themselves for reasons of professional jealousy. After all, why ruin a lucrative trick? What we do know is that the first proposal for getting airborne that had what we would now consider scientific merit was made by the English philosopher Roger Bacon in about 1250.

Roger Bacon (1214–92), a Franciscan friar from Ilchester in Somerset, was a Renaissance man before the event. The scope of his intellectual curiosity was so great that in 1266, Pope Clement IV commissioned him to write a compendium of the whole of human knowledge: the *Opus Majus*, or 'big book of everything'. Although he was – and this merely scratches the surface of his achievements – the inventor of the concept of spectacles and the first European to work out how to make gunpowder, Bacon's biggest contribution to science was probably his insistence on the experimental method. 'Cease to be ruled by dogmas and authorities; look at the world!' was his motto. (It was also his undoing: in 1277 he was imprisoned by the Church for 'certain novelties', and he remained in captivity until the year of his death.) This is ironic, because Bacon's greatest gifts now seem to have been imaginative: grasping principles, then envisaging how they might find practical application. One such imaginative leap was his intuition that the air had an upper surface on which it might be possible to sail a suitable craft: 'Such a machine must be a hollow globe of copper, or other suitable metal wrought extremely thin in order to have it as light as possible. This globe must be filled with aethereal air or liquid fire and launched into the atmosphere where it will float like a vessel on water.'

Nobody can be certain exactly what Bacon meant by 'aethereal air' and 'liquid fire'. The romantic interpretation is that he was correctly anticipating the eventual use of hydrogen and hot air as lifting agents. What is certain is that he was considerably ahead of his time in having any kind of grip on the true nature of air. It was almost four hundred years before the rest of the world finally caught up with him. Until then, air was not generally considered to be 'stuff' at all, at least in the conventional sense. It is easy to see with hindsight how, without that conceptual framework, would-be aeronauts hadn't much of a prayer.

The breakthrough came in 1643, when Evangelista Torricelli, an Italian mathematician and a former pupil of Galileo, decided to conduct some experiments with a quantity of quicksilver, or mercury, and a thin metal tube sealed at one end. He filled the tube with mercury, placed a finger over the open end and turned it upside down. Then he immersed his hand in a tray of mercury and released the finger. The mercury in the pipe did not seep out into the tray, but stood inside its tube in a proud column some thirty inches high. Torricelli reasoned that to support it, something must be pushing down on the contents of the tray. The only possible candidate was air.

When the French scientist Blaise Pascal heard about Torricelli's embryonic barometer, he decided to repeat the experiment. Unfortunately, he had no mercury to hand. What he did have access to, being French, was an abundant supply of red wine, so he improvised. But because wine is about fifteen times less dense than mercury, Pascal could not confirm Torricelli's discovery until he had constructed a barometer some forty feet high.

Once he had equipped himself with a more user-friendly set of mercury barometers, Pascal was ready to take the next step. If the atmosphere had a weight, he reasoned, logic dictated that it would decline with altitude. To test this hypothesis, he needed a mountain. Unfortunately, Pascal's home city of Paris was resolutely flat. To get round this problem, in 1648 he enlisted the services of his brother-in-law, Florin Périer, who lived in the volcanic Auvergne. While a sympathetic monk monitored a mercury barometer set up in Périer's garden, the owner set off with a similar device for the summit of the nearby Puy de Dôme (5396 feet). There he found his column of mercury to be some three inches shorter than its counterpart in the valley. Pascal's hunch had proved correct, and Roger Bacon's intuition that the atmosphere was a kind of ocean was confirmed.

It is a testament to Bacon's vision that the next 'viable' proposal for air travel, made by the Italian Jesuit Francesco de Lana-Terzi in 1670, was essentially just an elaboration of his own. However, instead of filling copper globes with aethereal air, liquid fire or anything else, Lana-Terzi planned to empty them. A vacuum, he reasoned, was lighter than any gas, and would correspondingly have more lift. Unfortunately, his proposal was even less practical than Bacon's: Lana-Terzi's evacuated copper globes would inevitably collapse under atmospheric pressure, whereas Bacon's would not – which the good friar had been smart enough to foresee.* Nonetheless, Lana-Terzi's musings restored comparative sanity to the pursuit of aerial flight. One popular contemporary theory had revolved around filling empty eggshells with morning dew. As

---

* There was a practical demonstration of this design flaw in 1843 when a certain M. Marey Monge took it upon himself to build a machine according to Lana-Terzi's specifications. It cost him 25,000 francs. Instead of copper, Monge chose to make his globes of brass, about four-thousandths of an inch thick. Having made his spheres, he lined each one with two thicknesses of tissue paper, varnished it with oil, and set to work emptying it of air. This, however, proved impossible, and the machine ended up as scrap metal.

the sun 'rarefied' the dew, the thinking went, the eggshells would rise, with anything that happened to be attached to them.

The first practical demonstration of a lighter-than-air flying machine occurred in 1709. In that year, a young Brazilian named Bartholemeu Lourenço de Gusmão petitioned the Portuguese king John V for the privilege of demonstrating to him his recent invention: an airship. Although it is unlikely that he ever built the fully fledged version of what he had in mind, an extravaganza of sails, bellows and magnets, he was granted a royal audience. It took place in the Casa da India palace in Lisbon on 8 August.

When the royal party was seated, Gusmão entered the hall with an apparatus consisting of a suspended earthenware bowl in which a fire had been kindled. He also produced a paper globe with an aperture at one end. He held this proto-balloon over the flames until it had filled with hot air, and then, marvellously, it began to rise. It mattered little that the small globe drifted towards some curtains, initiating a dramatic conflagration. The king was a satisfied man.

Alas, Gusmão was never able to capitalise on this promising start, despite continuing to conduct flying experiments for the rest of his life. In due course he fell foul of the Inquisition, and was forced to flee to Toledo in Spain, where he died in 1724.

In Gusmão, the world had come tantalisingly close to the birth of air travel. Another important step was taken by the French monk Galien, when he suggested in 1757 that a way be found to draw down lighter air from the upper reaches of the atmosphere. Captured in a suitable container, he argued, this could be used to pull a vessel aloft. Galien was nothing if not ambitious – he designed a craft capable of transporting four million passengers – but he was correspondingly impractical. The problem, in a nutshell, was one of circularity: to access the thin air required for its operation, a machine like the one he was proposing would have to exist already.

Evidently, man was going to need one more prod to get airborne. In the event, he would get it from the chemists.

———

Before the seventeenth century, western thought about the nature of matter was dominated by the Aristotelian doctrine of the four elements (the Chinese added a fifth, metal, to the list). All matter, with the important exception of that residing in the heavenly bodies, to which we will return, was believed to be made up, in various permutations, of earth, water, fire and air. Although Aristotle was keen to emphasise that no earthly substance was purely comprised of any one element, his theory had important consequences for the way in which the atmosphere was understood. For millennia, air was considered to be essentially indivisible and homogenous. Beyond that, little was known about its nature.

On an intuitive level, the four-element scheme had a great deal of appeal. We experience things in terms of their being solid, liquid, gaseous or hot-or-cold. But as people became more sophisticated in their manipulations of matter, particularly through the efforts of the medieval alchemists, the system came under increasing strain. To prop it up, three 'principles' were added to the list of elements: combustibility, fluidity and fixity (or incombustibility), represented respectively by sulphur, mercury and salt. Nevertheless, it was only a matter of time before the Aristotelian edifice collapsed. The man who blew it apart was Robert Boyle.

Boyle was an Old Etonian and the fourteenth child of the Earl of Cork. As a consequence, he never had to worry about money. This gave him full scope to purchase the exotic equipment and human assistance he needed to pursue his scientific interests. In the late 1650s, with the help of the inventor Robert Hooke, he constructed an air pump, which allowed him to explore the properties of this supposed element as nobody ever had before. Using this pump, he was able to demonstrate the crucial role of air in combustion, respiration and the transmission of sound (the latter through ringing a bell within an ever-increasing vacuum). He was also able to establish how it behaved under different conditions. The result was the law that bears his name: other things being equal, the volume of a gas is inversely proportional to the pressure applied to it. Three centuries on, this had important consequences for the designers of helium balloons.

While his work on air alone justifies his place in this story, Boyle had not finished. In 1661, he published *The Sceptical Chymist*, in which he attacked the Aristotelian system at its roots. The Greek elements, he argued, citing the evidence of his own experiments, could neither be combined to form other substances, nor could they be extracted from them. Therefore they couldn't be the building blocks of Nature. Instead, Boyle proposed that matter was made up of what he described as 'primary particles'. These he believed coalesced in various ways to form the substances of which the world was made. He called these coalitions 'corpuscles'. It would be left to others to distinguish between different kinds of primary particle, thereby redefining the word 'element', but the damage to the old concept had been done.

Despite his undoubted brilliance, Boyle never managed to put together the two and two of his theories about air and corpuscles to make the four that the atmosphere might be made up of different gases. That privilege was reserved for the eighteenth century. The process began in 1756, when the Scottish doctor Joseph Black published the results of some experiments he had carried out on magnesia alba (magnesium carbonate), ostensibly to investigate its suitability as a medicine for gastric complaints. On heating this material, he had found that a gas was produced that differed sharply in its characteristics from 'common air'. In particular, it was denser and it put out fire. Black was able to demonstrate both properties by 'pouring' the gas from a beaker over a naked flame, which was promptly extinguished. He called his new gas 'fixed air'. We now know it as carbon dioxide.

With Black's discovery, the notion that air was one indivisible substance was momentously exploded. Suddenly, scientists found themselves in a frantic race to discover other varieties of gas. At the forefront was another extremely wealthy aristocrat, the highly eccentric Henry Cavendish, grandson of the 2nd Duke of Devonshire.

Even to his friends, Henry Cavendish (1731–1810) was something of a mystery. One of them, Lord Brougham, opined that he 'probably uttered fewer words in the course of his life than any man who ever lived to fourscore years, not at all excepting the monks of La Trappe'. When he did speak, his voice was strange and shrill. He was painfully shy, particularly with women, and communicated with his housekeeper exclusively through written notes. Yet despite, or perhaps because of, this acute social unease, Cavendish immersed himself in scientific observation with unparalleled devotion. When he was on his deathbed, he asked to be left alone so that he could study the progress of his disease through his body uninterrupted.

In 1766, Cavendish repeated an earlier experiment by Robert Boyle in which sulphuric acid was added to iron, producing a very light and highly flammable gas. By taking careful measurements, he was able to prove that this gas had a considerably lower density than ordinary air. Because of its explosive properties, he called it 'flammable air'. Fifteen years later, he noticed that when flammable air was ignited, water was produced as a by-product. Because of this propensity, the gas became known as hydrogen, from the Ancient Greek for 'water-maker'.

Coal miners had long been indirectly aware of the existence of hydrogen through its sometimes lethal effects as they went about their work. But this was the first time it had been isolated and identified for what it was – not bad air or corrupted air, but a different gas. It was also, crucially, lighter than air. Here at last was the final piece of the jigsaw. In Cavendish's hydrogen, man had a substance worthy of Roger Bacon's copper globes, something truly capable of lifting him aloft. All that remained was for someone to build the machine that could utilise it.

Tiberius Cavallo, our friend from the beginning of the chapter, was quick to see the possibility of using hydrogen to persuade a suitable receptacle to float upwards. He tried various paper constructions, but found that the gas simply leaked through them. The best he could do for the moment was generate pleasingly explosive soap bubbles. Nevertheless, it seemed only a matter of time before hydrogen would be harnessed to build a flying machine. It was ironic, therefore, that the final impetus which propelled man skywards came from research into a different gas. It also came from some very dubious science.

According to the theory that was dominant for much of the eighteenth century, fire was not caused by anything in the air but by the loss of a mysterious substance from whatever was burning. This substance, which was believed to inhere in all flammable materials, was known as 'phlogiston'. Under the right circumstances, the theory held, an object would start to release its phlogiston into the surrounding air, causing it to burn. In the absence of outside interference, it would go on doing so until either it had released all its phlogiston, or the air around it had become saturated with the stuff.

When Cavendish first isolated hydrogen, he initially believed that it was pure phlogiston: the very principle of fire. A similar but opposite thought occurred in 1774 to Joseph Priestley, a nonconformist minister in both senses of the term, a passionate supporter of American Independence, and an amateur scientist of modest means. In the summer of that year, Priestley experimented with some gas he had collected while heating a sample of red mercuric oxide. When he lit a candle in it, he found that it burned 'with a remarkably vigorous flame'. What he had here, he reasoned, was air devoid of phlogiston – hence its ravenous hunger to suck it up. He therefore christened it 'dephlogisticated air'.

What Priestley had stumbled upon was oxygen. The same gas had been discovered the previous year by the Swedish apothecary Carl Wilhelm Scheele, but he had been too slow in publishing his findings to claim the credit. Priestley quickly got to work on his new substance, testing it among other things for its life-supporting qualities in mice. When he found that they survived up to three times longer than might be expected in ordinary air, he tried breathing some of it himself. 'I fancied that my breast felt peculiarly light and easy for some time afterwards,' he wrote. 'Who can tell but that, in time, this pure air may become a fashionable article in luxury? Hitherto,' he continued, 'only two mice and myself have had the privilege of breathing it.' Here, it would transpire, he was spectacularly wrong.

In 1775, Priestley had dinner with the great French chemist Antoine Lavoisier in Paris, and passed on his findings about oxygen. Lavoisier would go on to conduct experiments with the newly discovered gas that would not only show that it was an important component of the 'regular' atmosphere but would also repudiate the notion of phlogiston. Priestley clung to the discredited theory to the bitter end. Yet it was he and not the ostensibly better placed Cavendish or Lavoisier who gave mankind the long-awaited final push towards the heavens.

In 1776, Priestley's *Experiments and Observations on Different Kinds of Air* was published in French. In the small town of Annonay, a papermaker named Joseph Montgolfier got hold of a copy. What he did when he'd read and digested it changed the world for ever . . .

Chapter Three

THE REVOLUTION

In a field outside the village of Standon in Hertfordshire, there stands a stone monument with the following exultant inscription:

Let posterity know, and knowing be astonished, that on the fifteenth day of September, 1784, Vincent Lunardi of Lucca, in Tuscany, the first aerial traveller in Britain, mounting from the Artillery Ground in London, and traversing the regions of the air for two hours and fifteen minutes, on this spot revisited the earth. In this rude monument for ages be recorded this wondrous enterprise successfully achieved by the powers of chemistry and the fortitude of man, this improvement in science which the great Author of all Knowledge, patronising by his Providence the inventions of mankind, hath graciously permitted, to their benefit and his own eternal glory.

From the triumphant tone, you could be forgiven for assuming that the plaque commemorated a British invention. In fact, the technology that permitted Lunardi's journey belonged to Britain's deadliest rival, and at the time of his ascent, balloons had been flying over France for almost a year. It speaks volumes for the depth of feeling about the new invention that an English stonemason could still get so excited about it.

The man to whom it fell to first lift men from the Earth's surface was large, eccentric, and hilariously absent-minded. At various stages in his life, Joseph Montgolfier managed to leave both his wife and his horse behind when checking out of inns. A dreamer with a string of failed businesses behind him by the time he reached his forties, he had been too unconventional as a child to reap the benefits of a regular education so had grown up as the classic autodidact. The physical sciences in particular took his fancy. A cousin wrote that he was always 'torturing various substances with fire in order to achieve knowledge of them'.

Joseph (1740–1810) was the twelfth of sixteen children of Pierre Montgolfier, a wealthy paper manufacturer from Viladon-les-Annonay in the province of Vivrais in the South of France. An ancestor had set up the family business after returning from the Crusades at the end of the fourteenth century, having learned the secrets of papermaking while imprisoned in Damascus. Being something of a boffin himself, he had realised that paper could be made just as easily from old rags as from the expensive cotton used in the East. As a result, the business had flourished, eventually becoming Paper Manufactory by Appointment to the King. Nevertheless, by the early 1780s, the firm was suffering severely from an increase in competition. Something drastic was needed to restore the family's fortunes. In the event, it was provided by the clan's most oddball member.

Legends abound as to how Joseph Montgolfier first had the idea that led to the birth of the balloon. A popular theory suggests that he was inspired by the sight of his wife's bloomers billowing over the fireplace, inflated by heated air. Another favourite has it that the eureka moment occurred when a burning conical sugarloaf wrapper rocketed up the chimney. We know that the Montgolfiers were close neighbours of Galien, the monk who had dreamed of mass passenger air transport just a generation before. We also know that Montgolfier was well acquainted with the works of Priestley, whose gas experiments he had almost certainly duplicated. There is evidence that he was thinking on proto-balloon lines as early as 1777, when he interrogated a medical student cousin about what he had learned of gases. No doubt several different observations and experiences fed into Montgolfier's unconscious reckonings. But we have it on his authority that it all fell into place one evening in November 1782, while he was sitting in his lodgings in Avignon doing precisely nothing. (He had enrolled in the Avignon law faculty, which was effectively just a diploma mill, two years before.)

On the wall of the sitting room was a picture of the siege of Gibraltar, which France and Spain, determined to wrest the island fortress at the mouth of the Mediterranean from British control, had been conducting since June 1779. Just two months before the evening in question, the attacking forces had sustained terrible losses during a concerted effort to force a breakthrough. Joseph Montgolfier might have been an unworldly character, but he was also a patriot. As he stared at the picture, he fell into a reverie. Surely, he reasoned, there must be some way to get men on to the Rock. While he was mulling over the problem, his gaze fell on the fireplace, where some burning logs were sending sparks flying up the chimney. His eyes swivelled back to the picture, then back to the fire. Suddenly the penny dropped.

'I possess a superhuman means of introducing our soldiers into this impregnable fortress,' he would write shortly afterwards. 'They may enter through the air. The gas produced by the combustion of a little straw or a few rags should not pass, like the subtle inflammable air, through the pores of a paper bag. By making the bag large enough, it will be possible to introduce into Gibraltar an entire army, which, borne by the wind, will enter right above the heads of the English.'

Seized by this inspiration, Montgolfier rushed out to get himself some fine silk and a few sticks of extra-light wood He hastily constructed a frame, and stretched the material over it, leaving a small opening at one end. Hands sweating, he made some twists of paper, fixed them in the mouth of the device and then set fire to them. Immediately, he could feel the globe or *ballon* tugging upwards in his hands. Then he released it and, miraculously, it sailed up to the ceiling.

It would not have been atypical of Joseph Montgolfier if this experiment had ended with the entire street on fire. Instead, he calmly doused the flames and sat down to dash off a note to his younger brother, Étienne. 'Get in a supply of taffeta and rope, quickly,' he wrote, without elaborating, 'and you will see one of the most astonishing sights in the world.'

It was perhaps because the Montgolfier family was so large that it was able to provide the perfect foil for Joseph in the shape of child number fifteen. Étienne Montgolfier (1745–99) shared his brother's passionate nature, but that was about where the similarity ended. Where Joseph was chaotic, Étienne was focused and self-disciplined. He was a trained architect, and a cool-headed businessman. When the eldest brother, Raymond, had died a decade previously, it was Étienne who had taken charge of the family business, in defiance of his lowly place in the pecking order. Yet despite his pragmatic instincts, when he read Joseph's letter he dropped everything to do as his sibling requested.

Early in December 1782, the Montgolfier clan huddled outside the family home at Viladon to watch Joseph repeat his experiment. When, to their astonishment, his silk contraption rose to a height of some seventy feet, most family members were convinced that they need look no further for the potential solution to the financial problems of the paper business. Only the eighty-three-year-old Pierre begged to differ. He thought his sons had taken leave of their senses.

Over the next few months, the brothers worked ceaselessly

to improve the design of the new invention. They conducted three more tests in the countryside around Viladon, the third to a height of a thousand feet. Given the highly visible nature of the operation, it would have been a minor miracle if the secret hadn't leaked out, yet this is exactly what appears to have happened. For when the people of the area congregated in the small town square of Annonay (population 7000) on 4 June 1783 to witness the first public demonstration of the Montgolfiers' balloon, they did so with considerable scepticism.

The mood of doubt was only somewhat alleviated when the great and the good of the province of Vivrais began to file out of a nearby building to take their places in the Place des Cordeliers. It just so happened that the local diocesan assembly (the États Particuliers) was sitting in Annonay that week, and Étienne, with characteristic shrewdness, had deliberately timed the demonstration to take advantage of this. He was well aware of the need to get official recognition for the brothers' invention before anyone could steal the Montgolfier thunder.

The balloon at the centre of the hubbub was a spherical affair some 110 feet in circumference, made of cloth lined with paper and held together with 1800 buttons. At this stage, the standard method of inflation, whereby the source of heat is suspended beneath the mouth of the balloon, had yet to be invented. As a result, two men had to hold the opening over a fire to inflate the 'aerostatic machine' while somehow avoiding setting fire to either it or themselves.

As extraordinary as it may seem, Joseph Montgolfier was completely ignorant of the real reason for the success of his invention. Instead of recognising that air expands as it is heated, thus becoming less dense and therefore lighter than the unheated air around it, he believed that his balloon was propelled upwards by a special gas, obtained from the combustion of certain substances. As a consequence, much of his research time was taken up by a search for the perfect materials for the production of this gas. Currently, he favoured a mixture of straw and wool.

It is a profound truth of science that things sometimes work even if they are based on faulty reasoning. As Montgolfier threw finely judged quantities of wool and straw on to the fire, he might not have been producing phlogiston or hydrogen, but he was certainly producing hot air. As a result, the envelope swelled magnificently. By the time it was fully distended, eight men were struggling to hold it down. Not for the first time, and certainly not for the last, a tremendous advance was going hand in hand with a spurious understanding of why it was successful.

The crowd had been impressed enough when the balloon had inflated. When it was released, they were dumbfounded. 'The discordant minds of the spectators were instantly brought to an equal state of silent astonishment, which ended in loud and unfeigned acclamations,' as one contemporary author described it. The contraption sailed upwards into a menacing sky, climbing to around 6000 feet in a matter of minutes. Then it drifted slowly northwards, and gradually began to lose height. After ten gravity-defying minutes, the balloon made a gentle landing in a vineyard a mile and a quarter from the Place des Cordeliers. As Étienne explained soberly, 'The loss of gas through the buttonholes and other imperfections did not permit it to continue any longer.'

News of the events at Annonay was quick to reach Paris. The first published word on the subject, a rather scornful letter from a local landowner, did not hit the streets until 10 July, but by this stage the august Academy of Sciences was already aware of the Montgolfier experiment through the minutes of the Vivrais États Particuliers. For the élite scientists of the capital, the news that a pair of provincial papermakers had beaten them to this momentous discovery was difficult to swallow. To salvage its self-respect, the Academy was going to have to conduct a successful aerostatic experiment of its own, and soon. The question was, how had the Montgolfiers done it? To find out the answer, the Academy put one of its best young minds on to the problem.

Jacques Charles (1746–1823) was a flute-playing former civil servant who had taken up science after falling under the wing of Benjamin Franklin, the ambassador to France from the infant United States. As far as Charles was concerned, the only gas capable of providing the requisite lift was hydrogen, or 'inflammable air'. Indeed, he initially worked on the assumption that this was exactly what the Montgolfiers had used. The difficult part was finding a suitable material to contain the hydrogen, which had a habit of leaking out through the tiniest holes.

The solution to this dilemma was provided by the brothers Nicolas and Anne-Jean Robert, a pair of craftsmen who had perfected a technique of impregnating fabric with rubber. Immediately, Charles and the Roberts set to work in the courtyard of Charles' laboratory in the Place des Victoires, using some of this new material to construct a spherical balloon some twelve feet in diameter. Meanwhile, Charles' friend Faujas de Saint-Fond (who became the first great balloon impresario) opened a public subscription to finance the attempt in the Café de Caveau, just around the corner. One crown would purchase three prime tickets for the eventual launch.

A preliminary inflation of the *Globe*, as the Charles balloon was christened, was made on 23 August 1783. To generate the requisite hydrogen, iron was mixed with dilute sulphuric acid, or 'oil of vitriol', in a complicated apparatus that resembled a chest of drawers. Above this was suspended the rubberised silk envelope, connected to the hydrogen generator by a pipe.

Inflation was a slow and difficult process, with the heat of the reaction between acid and metal sending corrosive water vapour into the balloon, which had to be continually teased out as it condensed to prevent it burning through the fabric. At the end of the day, the *Globe* was only a third full of 'inflammable air'. Inflation was not completed until the following evening, by which stage a thousand pounds of iron and 498 pounds of sulphuric acid had already been consumed.

On 25 August, Charles and the Roberts conducted captive tests on the *Globe* to assess its lifting power. The next day, they allowed the balloon to rise to 100 feet. In retrospect, this was a mistake: at the sight of this unfamiliar object straining at its leash, an untenable crowd began to gather in the Place des Victoires, which the authorities only dispersed with the greatest difficulty. If the *Globe* was going to be such an irresistible people-magnet, clearly it was a non-starter to try to transport it to its launch site in the Champs de Mars by day. The only way it was ever going to get there was secretly, in the dead of night.

In the small hours of 27 August, the *Globe* was squeezed through the gateway from Charles' courtyard in a highly undignified manner. It was then tied to an ox cart, and led through Paris under armed guard, bobbing irrepressibly. This must have been quite a sight for the few night owls the cortège encountered. 'The nocturnal march, the form and the capacity of the body, carried with so much precaution; the silence that reigned, the unseasonable hour, all tended to give a singularity and mystery truly imposing to all those who were acquainted with the cause,' wrote Faujas de Saint-Fond. 'The cab-drivers on the road were so astonished that they were impelled to stop their carriages, and to kneel humbly, hat in hand, while the procession was passing.'

Given the potentially explosive combination of leaking

hydrogen and flaming torches, it was a triumph that the *Globe* ever reached the Champs de Mars at all. On arrival, it was tethered to a pair of iron stakes driven into the ground, and the laborious process of topping up began. All through the day, as people poured into the area, expectancy climbed exponentially. Then, at 5 p.m., a single cannon shot was fired, and the *Globe* was released. Simultaneously, rain began to fall sharply, but not a soul in the vast audience seemed to notice. They were too busy staring upwards, transfixed: within two minutes, the *Globe* had soared to 3000 feet. The crowd groaned as it disappeared into a raincloud, then cheered as it reappeared to the sound of another cannon shot. Every eye in the city followed it as it drifted in and out of the clouds all the way to the horizon.

Forty-five minutes later, the *Globe* landed fifteen miles away in a field near the village of Gonesse (coincidentally the site of the Air France Concorde disaster of 2000). The terrified villagers congregated around the balloon with scythes and pitchforks, believing it to be something demonic, or an escapee from another world. When they had plucked up enough courage, they attacked it. According to a Paris journal, 'The creature, shaking and bounding, dodged the first blows. Finally, however, it received a mortal wound, and collapsed with a long sigh.' The stench of sulphuric acid and hot rubber must have been horrendous. When the villagers were quite sure the monster was dead, they tied it to a horse's tail, and sent the animal galloping away across the fields.

Although they have been widely ridiculed ever since, it is easy to feel some sympathy for the residents of Gonesse. After all, what could they have been expected to think? As we shall see, people were still inclined to invest unfamiliar balloon debris with extraterrestrial origins as late as the 1950s. In any case, the French government wisely decided to issue a proclamation to pre-empt panic, even before it learned of the *Globe*'s eventual fate:

Announcement to the people on the ascent of balloons or globes in the air. The one in question has been raised in Paris this said day, 27 August 1783, at 5 p.m., in the Champ de Mars.

A discovery has been made, which the Government deems it right to make known, so that alarm be not occasioned to the people.

On calculating the different weights of inflammable and common air, it has been found that a balloon filled with inflammable air will rise towards heaven until it is in equilibrium with the surrounding air. This may not happen until it has reached a great height.

The first experiment was made at Annonay in Vivrais by the inventors Messieurs Montgolfier; a globe formed of canvas and paper, 105 feet in circumference, filled with inflammable air, reached an uncalculated height.

The same experiment has just been repeated in Paris (27 August at 5 p.m.) in the presence of a great crowd. A globe of taffeta, covered by elastic gum, 36 feet in circumference, has risen from the Champ de Mars, and been lost to view in the clouds, being borne in a northeasterly direction; it is impossible to foresee where it will descend.

It is proposed to repeat these experiments on a larger scale. Anyone who sees such a globe (which resembles a darkened moon) in the sky should be aware that, far from being an alarming phenomenon, it is only a machine, made of taffeta, or light canvas covered with paper, which cannot possibly cause any harm and which will some day prove serviceable to the wants of society.

Despite its savage treatment at the hands of the villagers, Charles was able to diagnose from the *Globe*'s wreckage that the balloon must have burst before landing. He correctly attributed this to the enclosed hydrogen expanding due to altitude. In future, gas balloons would be equipped with open necks to prevent repeat performances.

————

Throughout the late summer and autumn of 1783, Paris was gripped by a mania for all things balloon. In early September, a craze broke out for miniature versions made of goldbeaters' skin (cattle gut), which could be inflated by hydrogen generated at home. According to Tiberius Cavallo, these nine- to eighteen-inch novelties 'began to be manufactured by those who were anxious to derive a pecuniary profit from the improvements of philosophy; and as the price of these balloons did not exceed a few shillings, almost every family satisfied its curiosity relative to the new experiment, and in a few days' time balloons were seen very frequently about Paris, and soon after were sent abroad'. Balloon motifs appeared on snuff-boxes, fans and sword-hilts. Birdcages, chandeliers, even hairstyles were constructed in shapes that mimicked the new obsession. There was only one topic of conversation that season. 'Balloons occupy senators, philosophers, ladies, everybody,' wrote the British statesman Horace Walpole. A cocktail was invented to celebrate the great invention: Crème Aerostatique. There was even a new dance, the Contredanse de Gonesse.

Although Charles and the Robert brothers appeared for the moment to have stolen the initiative, Étienne Montgolfier was busily preparing to wrest it back. He had travelled to Paris as early as 11 July, intent on securing recognition for his family's discovery, while the shy Joseph hid himself away in Lyon. Shortly after his departure, another brother, Jean-Pierre, had dispatched a letter after him, informing Étienne that their aged father, who had hitherto refused to have anything to do with the project, had relented. Pierre Montgolfier now wanted his son to know that, in his youth, his own father had taught him a trick: empty an egg through a small hole pricked in one end, seal it up with a tiny blob of wax, heat the eggshell over a stove, and it will fly up to the ceiling. Somehow, Montgolfier *grandpère* had reached the same conclusion as the Chinese author almost two thousand years before.

Étienne had tried to inform the Academy of Sciences of Joseph's discovery the previous winter, writing to an acquaintance who was a member to outline the main features of the invention, and to complain that 'we are surrounded by hornets and they will not hesitate to steal our work and appropriate the credit'. On hearing this news, the contact had understandably elected to keep it quiet. As soon as Étienne arrived in Paris, he set about putting that right. His first move was to enlist the help of an old client from his architectural days, Monsieur Réveillon, wallpaper manufacturer to the king. He pitched camp in the garden of Réveillon's factory in the Faubourg St Antoine, and set about constructing an enormous and curiously shaped blue and gold balloon, more than 40 feet in diameter and 70 feet high. Meanwhile, the pair began to exploit their connections to set up demonstrations before the Academy (14 September) and then before King Louis XVI himself (19 September). By the time the Charles *Globe* was launched, Étienne had already secured government finance for his project.

The demonstration before the Academy was not a great success. It began well enough, when the balloon, which was made of packing linen sandwiched between two layers of paper, inflated gratifyingly quickly in comparison with the Charles version. Then, unfortunately, a storm broke, snatching the balloon in a sudden gust. It was laboriously hauled back to Earth against the pull of the wind, but was damaged in the process. A moment later the heavens opened, and the whole thing was reduced to a sodden mess.

It was now all hands to the pump at the Réveillon factory

to get a new balloon ready for Versailles. Montgolfier decided that this should be a somewhat smaller and simpler version of its predecessor. Work continued round the clock, and by 18 September, the replacement balloon was ready for its trial inflation. It was transported to Versailles with considerably less fuss than had attended the cross-town journey of the *Globe*.

On the day of the launch, a crowd of up to 130,000 eager spectators thronged the vicinity of Versailles. Inside the palace, Étienne Montgolfier sat down to a magnificent banquet, then set about inflating the balloon, which was suspended over a hollow octagonal stage in the courtyard. To make the requisite gas, the usual wool and straw were burned together, but this time some old shoes and some pieces of decomposed meat were added as well. This was all too much for the sensitive noses of Louis XVI and Marie-Antoinette, who came to inspect the machine then rapidly withdrew.

It had long been the Montgolfiers' intention to trump Charles at Versailles with the successful transportation of living beings. At this stage, however, human passengers were out of the question. Although it had always been the ultimate, if often unspoken, aim to use the new technology to get people aloft, it was felt that as yet far too little was known about the effects of altitude to justify taking the risk. The prevailing view was that creatures designed for the surface of the Earth were likely to fare as badly when they tried to survive in the realm of the birds as they would in the kingdom of the fishes.

The fear of suffocation that surrounded the first balloon ascents might seem strange to us now. After all, people had already climbed mountains taking them a great deal higher than a few thousand feet above Versailles and lived to tell the tale. It seems that despite the previous century's discovery of the weight of the atmosphere, air was still widely believed to be more like an aura or halo than an 'ocean'. As a result, distance above the surface rather than absolute altitude was thought to be what mattered.

In the end, it was agreed that the first aeronauts should be dumb animals, just as dogs and monkeys eventually had the dubious honour of becoming our first emissaries in space. Family correspondence in the run-up reveals a lively debate about which particular species to use as guinea-pigs. One brother, the Abbé Alexandre, argued the merits of a dog because of the noise it would make up in the air. Joseph was in favour of a cow on the grounds of greater visibility. In the end, however, the three beasts chosen to make this leap into the unknown were a cockerel, a duck and a sheep. History fails to relate exactly why the Montgolfiers settled on this line-up. The most likely explanation is that it reflected a desire to contrast the fates of a thoroughly terrestrial mammal, a terrestrial creature that also happened to be a bird (the chicken) and a bird thoroughly used to flight (the duck) when exposed to the upper regions of the atmosphere. When analysed, these could be expected to yield vital information about what worked up there and why.

At all events, to the now customary amazement of the spectators, the balloon and its farmyard cargo were eventually launched to a countdown of three cannon shots. According to two astronomers from the palace observatory, they rose to a height of 1700 feet. Meanwhile, as Étienne wrote in a letter to his wife: 'I went right up to the royal apartments and found the king still engaged in observing the machine with his field glasses. He showed me the locality where it had fallen, expressed his satisfaction, and at my request gave orders that people go to the place where it lay stranded to verify the condition of the animals.'

The first to the scene in the forest of Vaucresson some mile and a quarter distant was a twenty-six-year-old named Pilâtre de Rozier. He arrived to find the sheep grazing placidly and the duck in fine fettle, but the cockerel appeared to have damaged a wing. A heated debate ensued as to whether or not this injury had been caused by exposure to altitude. The issue was resolved when several witnesses swore that they had seen the sheep kick the bird just prior to take-off.

Little is known about the subsequent career of the duck and the cockerel, but we do know that the sheep lived out a happy retirement at Marie-Antoinette's play farm at Le Hameau. Étienne Montgolfier, meanwhile, spent the rest of the day being fêted at the palace. Among the whirl of individuals to whom he was introduced was a man who had composed a poem in his honour. It began with the line 'The creator of this globe is still merely a mortal man'.

The next step was to send a person up there.

————

Immediately after the Versailles demonstration, the Mont-golfier team returned to Réveillon's garden to get to work on the vehicle that would bear man on his maiden voyage to the skies. This balloon was ovoid in shape, approximately 75 feet high and 50 feet in diameter, with a neck 16 feet across. Around this was a wicker walkway, a yard in width, sewn to the main envelope by numerous small cords. This curved to form a slightly higher balustrade on its outside. Beneath the neck was a fire basket, held in place by iron chains, which could be fed with fuel from the walkway through special openings in the side of the balloon.

The choice of what constituted suitable decoration for the vessel entrusted with the solemn journey ahead tells us much about the gravity with which the participants viewed their task. It was just as well Réveillon was in the habit of making grandiose wallpaper. The background of the balloon was blue, in tribute to the element it hoped to enter. Around the top were the twelve signs of the zodiac, painted in gold, and again reflecting the celestial destination. Then, continuing downwards, there were bands of fleur-de-lis, royal ciphers alternating with Sun motifs, lions' faces and garlands. At the base, four giant painted eagles supported the balloon with their outstretched wings.

We know from an anxious letter from his wife that at some point Étienne himself must have conducted a tethered test of the balloon. This is also the implication of a letter from Jean-Pierre, in which old Pierre Montgolfier had him convey the message that 'He requires you to give him no further cause for distress and . . . not to get into the machine.' Whether or not for the sake of filial obedience, Étienne eventually decided to make way for a younger man. There was one obvious candidate: Pilâtre de Rozier, the winner of the race to the duck, cock and sheep.

Pilâtre de Rozier was born in Metz, where he was apprenticed as an adolescent to a prominent apothecary. He eventually ran away to Paris, where he wound up as the impresario of a museum of popular science (a sort of eighteenth-century Disneyland) under the patronage of the king's brother and sister-in-law. Although his grasp of science was tenuous, de Rozier was charming and he was courageous. A favourite trick of his was to inhale hydrogen then ignite it as he blew it out through a straw. He also had endurance: he had once immersed himself in excrement in a gas-filled sewer for thirty-four hours to demonstrate the effectiveness of a breathing apparatus he had invented for the city's benighted sewage workers.

According to legend, de Rozier only put himself forward when he heard that the king had insisted that the test subjects of any manned attempt must be convicted criminals. 'Eh, quoi! De villains criminels auraient la gloire de s'élever dans les airs les premiers! Non, non, cela ne sera point,' he is supposed to have said ('No way am I going to let two vile criminals have the glory of being the first men to fly through the air'). To that end, he enlisted the help of the Marquis d'Arlandes, who promised to press de Rozier's case at court, provided that he was allowed to accompany him on the forthcoming flight. D'Arlandes in turn had an influential friend in the person of the Duchesse de Polignac, governess to the royal children, who persuaded Marie-Antoinette to plead the pair's case before the king. Louis gave his consent, and a date was set: 21 November.

Before this could happen, of course, the balloon had to be subjected to a ruthless testing process. On 15 October, de Rozier arrived at the Réveillon factory, and stepped rather gingerly into the gallery. The balloon rose a few feet, then tipped over violently towards its startled occupant. This instability was quickly corrected by placing 110 pounds of ballast on the other side. De Rozier then rose up to 84 feet, the full extent of the tethering rope, and managed to stay there for four and a half minutes by feeding the furnace. He then descended gracefully, and would have made a textbook landing, had he not, in his excitement, ruined the effect by climbing out of the gallery before the balloon had been tied down. Naturally, it shot back up again, but was fortunately restrained by the tethering rope.

For the remainder of the day, de Rozier conducted further tests, refining the technique of controlling the height of the balloon through adding alcohol-soaked straw to the fire. Two days later, a large crowd had mysteriously gathered (there had been no advertisement), only to be disappointed when de Rozier cancelled his planned testing due to windy conditions. Then, on 19 October, de Rozier made four captive ascents which convinced all concerned that a free flight was a viable proposition. First, he rose to a height of 210 feet, and stayed there for six minutes. Then he went up to 262 feet. During his descent, he demonstrated his new-found skill by avoiding landing in a tree in the adjoining garden at the last possible moment, simply by tossing a little fuel into the furnace. Next, de Rozier was joined by a passenger, an employee of the Réveillon firm named Girond de Villette. This time, he took the balloon to the full extent of the rope – a height of 314 feet. Finally, he repeated the process with the Marquis d'Arlandes. At this height, the balloon was visible over much of Paris, and the sight of it generated feverish excitement.

The day before the balloon was scheduled to take off from the Château de la Muette, seat of the two-year-old Dauphin, an enormous crowd descended on the surrounding Bois de Boulogne, solely on the strength of a rumour. The news that they had arrived twenty-four hours early was not well received. November 21 was a windy day, and the sky, poised to receive its first human visitors, was filled with great white cumulus clouds. De Rozier made a trial ascent, in the course of which the balloon was damaged by a strong gust of wind, the problem being compounded by the resistance of the tethering rope. The huge crowd that had again assembled grew dangerously restless, a phenomenon that was a frequent hazard at balloon launches for years to come. Fortunately, if the aristocratic ladies in the central enclosure were good for one practical thing, it was sewing. Within two hours, the torn balloon was declared fit for use.

The sumptuous *Montgolfière* took to the air at 1.54 p.m. Its progress was stately rather than dramatic, and the entire flight took place at low altitude, possibly as a result of the damage sustained earlier in the day. But what was taking place was of incalculable significance, and this was not lost on the astonished crowd.

D'Arlandes later wrote a narrative of the expedition, in the form of a letter addressed to Faujas de Saint-Fond who, continuing his self-appointed role as champion of the balloon, had organised it:

I wish to describe as well as I can the first journey which men have attempted through an element which, prior to the discovery of MM. Montgolfier, seemed so little fitted to support them.

We ascended on the 21st of October, 1783, at almost two o'clock, with M. Rozier on the west side of the balloon and myself on the east. The wind was roughly north-west. The public say that the machine rose with majesty; but in reality the position of the balloon shifted so that M. Rozier was in front and I was in the rear.

I was surprised by the stillness and silence of the spectators, and believed them to be astonished and perhaps alarmed by the strange spectacle. They need not have worried. I was still gazing, when M. Rozier cried to me: 'You are doing nothing, and the balloon is scarcely rising a fathom.' 'Pardon me,' I answered, as I placed a bundle of straw upon the fire and stirred it slightly. Then I turned around, but already we had passed out of sight of La Muette. Astonished, I cast a glance towards the river. I could see the confluence of the Oise. And as I could identify the principal bends of the river by the places nearest them, I shouted out their names: 'Passy, St Germain, St Denis, Sèvres!'

'If you keep looking at the river in that fashion you will be swimming in it soon,' cried Rozier. 'Fire, my dear friend, fire!'

We travelled on, but instead of crossing the river directly, we veered towards Les Invalides, and then moved back over the centre of the river again. We continued beyond the barrier of La Conférence in this manner, zigzagging above the river but never crossing it.

'That river is very difficult to cross,' I remarked to my companion.

'So it seems,' he answered, 'but I see that you are not doing anything. You must be braver than me, and not afraid of falling in.'

I stirred the fire, seized a bundle of straw with my fork, lifted it up, and threw it into the middle of the flames. Immediately, I felt myself lifted towards the heavens.

'At last we are moving,' I said.

'Yes, we're moving,' answered my companion.

At that moment, I heard a noise from the top of the balloon that made me think it had burst. I looked up, but couldn't see anything. My companion had climbed inside it, no doubt to make some observations. While I was staring at the top of the machine, I felt a shock, the only one to date. The direction of the movement was downwards.

'What are you doing? Are you dancing up there?' I asked.

'I'm not moving.'

'So much the better. It must just be a new current of wind which I hope will carry us from the river,' I answered.

I turned to see where we were, and found we were between the École Militaire and the Invalides.

'We are getting on,' said Rozier.

'Yes, we are travelling.'

'Back to work, back to work,' he said.

I now heard another report in the machine, which I thought might have been produced by the snapping of a cord. This suspicion made me carefully examine the inside of our new home. I saw that the part facing south was full of holes, some of a considerable size.

'We've got to go down,' I cried.

'Why?'

'Look!' I said. At the same time I took my sponge and quietly extinguished some small flames that were burning some of the holes within my reach, but at the same moment I noticed that the bottom of the cloth was coming away from the circle that surrounded it.

'We must descend,' I repeated to my companion.

He looked below.

'We are over Paris,' he said.

'It doesn't matter,' I answered. 'Take a look! Do you not call this danger? Are you holding on well?'

'Yes.'

I then looked out from my side, and saw that in fact we had nothing to fear. I then tried all the ropes within reach with my sponge. All of them held firm. Only two of the cords had broken.

I then said, 'We can cross Paris.'

During this operation we were rapidly descending towards the roofs. We made more fire, and rose again with the greatest ease. I looked down, and it seemed we were going towards the towers of St Sulpice; but, on rising, a new current made us quit this direction and bear more to the south. I looked to the left, and saw a wood, which I believed to be the Luxembourg Gardens. As we were crossing the boulevard, I cried out: 'Brace yourself!'

But the intrepid Rozier, who never lost his head, and who was a better judge than me, prevented me from attempting to descend. I then threw a bundle of straw on the fire. We were now close to the ground, between two mills. As soon as we came near the earth I raised myself over the gallery, and leaning there with my two hands, I felt the balloon pressing softly against my head. I pushed it back, and leaped down to the ground. Looking round and expecting to see the balloon still distended, I was astonished to find it quite empty and flattened. I looked for Rozier, and saw him in his shirt-sleeves, creeping out from under the mass of canvas that had fallen over him. Before attempting to descend he had put off his coat and placed it in the basket. After a great deal of trouble we were finally all right.

As Rozier was without a coat, I begged him to go to the nearest house. On his way there, he ran into the Duke of Chartres, who must have followed us very closely, for I had had the honour of talking with him just before we set out.

Even the official observers, in their coldly scientific report, admitted to feelings of 'mingled fear and admiration' when de Rozier and d'Arlandes had bowed their heads to the multitude shortly after take-off. One of the signatories to the report was Benjamin Franklin. During the ascent, it is said, someone in his party commented that ballooning was all very well, but what was the use of it? 'What use is a newborn baby?' Franklin replied, unanswerably.

———

Two days before the historic voyage from the Château de la Muette, the Charles camp had opened a public subscription in the *Paris Journal* to finance a manned ascent of its own. Again, it was proposed that two men participate in the flight, but this time they would be the vehicle's creators. The third and fourth men in the sky would be Jacques Charles and the elder Robert brother, Nicolas.

On 1 December 1783, Paris came to a complete standstill as half the population gathered to witness the launch of the Charles balloon. Centred on the Tuileries garden, where the élite had gathered at a price of ninety-six livres a head, a vast multitude spilled out to the horizon. Every conceivable vantage-point was exploited: the city's bridges, riverbanks and rooftops all swarmed with spectators. The crowd was estimated at 400,000 individuals, the largest in the history of the world to date.

The balloon at the epicentre of all this was a perfect sphere, 27½ feet in circumference, and as coldly geometrical as the Montgolfiers' creations were baroque. To the citizens of eighteenth-century France, it must have seemed as futuristic and alien as a spaceship. Its sole adornment was a colour scheme of red and yellow stripes. Perhaps to compensate for this fact, the wickerwork gondola beneath it was wildly over the top, with golden pinion-feathers, fleur-de-lis and a crown on its stern. It was also asymmetrical, which made it highly unbalanced.

Charles was a quick learner and, accordingly, had introduced a number of innovations for the flight. In the first place, he wisely elected to inflate the balloon some way from the launch site to avoid inflaming the impatience of the spectators. It was suspended from a pair of trees in the Grand Avenue, and filled using a greatl improved system in which several barrels of iron and acid fed into a single umbilicus. The lessons of Gonesse had also been absorbed, and this balloon was equipped with valves at both top and bottom to allow the siphoning off of excess hydrogen. Equally important was the introduction of the procedure of balancing, in which sandbags were removed from the fully laden gondola

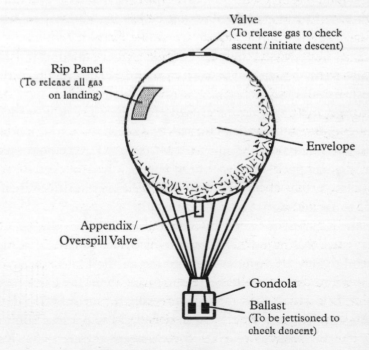

BASIC ANATOMY OF A GAS BALLOON

just prior to launch until the balloon was in a precise state of equilibrium. In this way, provided the pilots were judicious in their removal of ballast, the rate of ascent could be carefully controlled.

There was one more novelty in the run-up to take-off, and it provided a welcome opportunity to bury a rumour that had marred the early days of the balloon. From the outset, the press had tried to stir up enmity between the Charles and Montgolfier camps, claiming for instance that Étienne had been turned away from the Champs de Mars demonstration for not having a ticket. In fact, Charles had always acknowledged his debt to the Montgolfiers, and Faujas de Saint-Fond had even opened one of his public subscriptions to pay for a medal commemorating the brothers. Nevertheless, it was a touching moment when Charles handed a small green trial balloon to Étienne Montgolfier just before the launch. 'It is for you, sir, to show us the way to the skies,' he said, with a bow. Montgolfier released the trial balloon, which sailed upwards and to the north-east. Then Charles and Robert climbed on board, removed a sandbag, and took off after it.

It takes a lot to silence a crowd of 400,000, but the events of the next few seconds achieved it. The balloon rose like a bubble in a bottle of champagne (with which the gondola was liberally equipped), and within moments it had reached 1800 feet. Then Charles and Robert waved flags to indicate their well-being and a vast roar broke out below.

Later Charles described his initial sensations: 'Nothing will ever match that moment of hilarity which filled my whole being when I felt myself flying away from the Earth. It was not mere pleasure; it was perfect bliss.' 'I don't care about the Earth any more,' he declared to Robert. 'It's the sky for me now!'

Anyone who has ever been in a balloon will know something of the feelings of elation that swept through Charles and Robert at that moment. As they drifted on the breeze, surrendered to and therefore at one with it, it seemed as if they were hanging motionless, while the Earth flew and twisted down beneath them. They must have felt like gods as they soared over the face of the waters of the Seine. Perhaps this was what death would be like, when the soul, liberated from the confines of the flesh, would be free to fly where it pleased.

Fifty-six minutes into the flight, a cannon shot told the delirious occupants of the balloon that they had now passed out of view of the Tuileries. One hour later, Charles valved gas to execute a perfect landing just outside the town of Nesle, twenty-seven miles from the point of departure. For some time, a group of peasants had been chasing the balloon 'like children pursuing a butterfly', but the first to the scene was an Englishman named Farrer, who owned a nearby hunting lodge. He ran up to Charles and flung his arms round him. 'Monsieur Charles, I was here first!' he cried.

After much handshaking with residents of Nesle, Charles was seized by a desire to get back in the balloon. It is possible that he wanted to take the opportunity to bag the honour of first solo aeronaut for himself. At any rate, noting that the envelope was now 'quite soft and flabby', he severely underestimated how much lift it had retained. In the absence of the ballast that was Nicolas Robert, the balloon shot upwards, reaching a height of 10,000 feet within minutes. Charles suddenly found himself in a curious and extremely chilly world above the clouds, where he 'saw nothing but a wide expanse of fine aether'. The Sun, which had set for the rest of France some minutes earlier, now seemed to have risen again: 'I stood up in the middle of the gondola and lost myself in the spectacle offered by the immensity of the horizon. When I took off from the fields, the Sun had set for the inhabitants of the valleys. Soon it rose for me alone, and again appeared to gild the balloon and gondola with its rays.' Then, as an encore, it set once more.

Isolated above a sea of fog, and experiencing a silence more profound than any mortal had before, Charles underwent a moment of self-knowledge. The blood rushing through his veins was clearly audible. 'I could hear myself live, so to speak,' he would later say.

Two factors shook Charles back into the realms of practical reality. The first was the need to take scientific measurements: the atmospheric pressure, he found, had fallen by almost a third, and the temperature by 30 degrees Fahrenheit. The second consideration was a sudden sharp pain in his right ear and jawbone. In the uniqueness of his position, Charles must have been terrified. For all he knew, his head was about to explode. He wasted no time in beginning his descent, but retained the presence of mind to produce another perfect landing.

In his writings on the subject of his solo ascent, Charles comes across as relatively blasé. In truth, the experience must have been overwhelming for him. Circumstantial evidence certainly points in that direction: Jacques Charles, pioneer extraordinary, never went up in a balloon again . . .

———

It is difficult to exaggerate the impression that those first ascents made on those who witnessed them.

Shortly after Charles and Robert's take-off, inside the palace of the Tuileries, the old Maréchal Villeroi, an octogenarian invalid who did not believe in balloons, was conducted to one of the windows almost by force. When he saw Charles and Robert ascending in their sky-boat, he fell on his knees and burst into tears. 'Yes, it is fixed! It is certain!' he moaned. 'They will find out the secret of avoiding death; but it will be after I am gone!'

With the bonds of gravity broken, people suddenly felt freed from the human condition. Now that man had so demonstrably transcended his station in life, it seemed that anything was possible. This belief would be spectacularly confirmed within seven years by another revolution sweeping through the country. Again, huge expectant crowds would gather to see a complete reversal in the way of things.

Perhaps Sultan Murat had been right when he banished the precocious Hezarfen Celebi. Maybe it really was dangerous for the powers-that-be to have people flying about the place. As man ventured into the sky, it was inevitable that he would develop a new perspective on the world, both literally and metaphorically. It was only natural that he might come to act on it.

The conquest of the skies also spelled danger for traditional religion, as the God of the Tower of Babel story had anticipated. If people were going to start climbing into the heavens, it was inevitable that his position would come under threat – particularly, at least in the minds of the more literal-minded, when they didn't find anyone up there. Ballooning might have been only one in a series of setbacks for the old kind of faith, but it was a significant one nevertheless. Human beings now had access to both a viewpoint and a mode of travel (ascension) that had hitherto been exclusively reserved for the divine.

For now, the deeper consequences of the invention of the balloon remained in the future. The pioneers of the new sport busied themselves with establishing a series of firsts. On 24 February 1784, the first manned ascent outside France took place at Moncuco in Italy. In June of that year, in Lyon, the first woman took to the air, a Madame Thible, singing as she went. Then on 7 January 1785, Jean-Pierre Blanchard and John Jeffries became the first balloonists to cross the Channel. They made it to France by the skin of their teeth and naked, having been forced to shed their clothing *en route* to keep their balloon a few critical inches above the waves.

The party ended abruptly in June 1785, when Pilâtre de Rozier was killed while attempting to cross the Channel from Calais with his friend Pierre-Jules Romain. In building the balloon in which they were travelling, a hybrid device consisting of a hydrogen envelope on top of a cylinder of hot air, de Rozier had effectively constructed a bomb. Predictably, it caught fire and exploded. Both men were killed instantly, and the balloon crashed near Boulogne. Thus the first man to go up in a balloon became the first man to die in one, and the sky had claimed victims number one and two.

Chapter Four

HOLLOMAN

Around the middle of the 1950s, a series of strange objects began to plunge from the vast desert skies of New Mexico in the south-western United States. In broad terms, these visitors resembled human beings – they were similar in size, with the familiar distribution of limbs and head – but in other respects they were disconcertingly different. Particularly in their strange, wide-eyed expressions, and the fact that some had instrument panels spilling from their crushed skulls and midriffs.

Those who came across these figures noticed that they were invariably connected to parachutes. Some appeared to have deployed successfully, but the majority had wrapped perniciously around their hosts, causing them to crash to Earth at great speed. Clearly, these beings must have left whatever craft had transported them in some kind of emergency. Equally clearly, their escape systems were not well adapted to terrestrial conditions. The obvious inference was that they were visitors from another planet.

America's burgeoning fascination with space during the fifties went deeper than a vogue for sci-fi films of the *It Came From Outer Space* variety. At one level, the preoccupation derived from the fact that terrestrial opportunities for exploration were now largely exhausted, as the conquest of Mount Everest in May 1953 had confirmed. The pioneering spirit on which the USA was premised urgently needed new territory to chew on, and the only place to go was upwards. A similar impulse had lain behind the building of the first skyscrapers.

Now small children put away their cowboys and Indians and started to play with spacemen and aliens instead.

If there was a joyful dimension to this new expression of the frontier mentality, there was also a darker side to the equation: the technological advances that made space travel and all other kind of marvels seem so tantalisingly plausible were also profoundly unsettling. In the context of the Cold War, they were terrifying. Entire populations were seized by an amorphous but persistent sense of dread, the true origin of which, for many, was too awful to contemplate. From the moment the Soviet Union exploded its first atom bomb in the summer of 1949, the sky took on a menacing new aspect. Who knew what might descend at any moment from above? Little wonder that the temptation was strong to pin the anxiety on aliens from outer space. And nowhere was it stronger than in New Mexico.

The citizens of the Tularosa Basin in the south of the state had more reason than most for a touch of Cold War paranoia. This was not merely because the mountain-fringed wasteland in which they lived directed the eye irresistibly towards the sky: it was there, at 5.29 a.m. on 16 July 1945, that the world had entered the nuclear age, with the detonation of the first atomic weapon at the so-called Trinity Site, thirty-five miles west of the dusty township of Carrizozo, in the stretch of desert known as the Journada del Muerto ('journey of death'). Yet momentous as this event was, it was only one among many highly classified military projects to be conducted in the yucca- and saltbush-strewn scrubland of this vast, empty valley. Among them was the infant American rocket programme.

The roots of this programme lay in Nazi Germany. As early as 1936, a team of scientists, headed by a visionary pyromaniac named Wernher von Braun, had been assembled on the remote Baltic island of Peenemunde to develop the weapons which the Nazis hoped would lead them to world domination. The eventual fruit of their labours was the A4 rocket, later to be infamously renamed the V2. In its first successful test, the missile had climbed to the unprecedented altitude of sixty miles, following its planned trajectory precisely before landing some 120 miles from the point of launch. The occasion had moved General Walter Dornberger, the military overseer of the project, to issue the following triumphant proclamation: 'We have invaded space with our rocket and for the first time – mark this well – we have used space as a bridge between two points on the Earth. This third day of October 1942, is the first of a new era of transportation, that of space travel.'

Fortunately for the Allies, the V2 had arrived too late to win the war for the Germans. By the time the weapon was ready to be fired in anger (it made its début on 8 September 1944, landing and exploding in Staveley Road in Chiswick), the pendulum had swung irrevocably towards the other side. After Hitler's suicide, von Braun and over a hundred of his colleagues hid themselves away in the Haus Ingeburg inn near the town of Oberjoch in the Bavarian Alps, waiting for the end to come. Before his death, Hitler had ordered all the Peenemunde scientists executed, to ensure that their secrets never fell into the hands of the Allies. Their destiny now hinged on who would get to them first: the Americans, the Russians, or their own murderous colleagues from the SS.

In the event, von Braun and his team were able to make contact with the US forces, and on 2 May 1945, the day that Berlin fell to the Soviet Army, the scientists crossed to American lines. Their new captors interrogated and jealously guarded their prime human booty as the Russians looked on covetously. Then they set about supplementing it with hardware. Enough rocket parts were collected to allow the construction of some 100 working V2s, which were shipped across the Atlantic along with the hastily vetted scientists. By February 1946, a *doppelgänger* Peenemunde had sprung up near the Holloman Air Force Base just outside the town of Alamogordo in White Sands, New Mexico, a short hop across the desert from the site of the recent nuclear explosion.

Over the next few years, residents of the Tularosa Basin grew as accustomed as anyone can to the sights and sounds of large lumps of metal screaming into the sky. On 16 April 1946, the first V2 was launched from American soil. Three years later, a rocket fired from White Sands missile range climbed 244 miles into space, reaching a speed of 5510 miles per hour, the greatest altitude and velocity yet attained by a man-made object. The rocket programme subsequently moved on, to Cape Canaveral in Florida, but there were plenty of other shadowy research projects to take its place. Intriguingly, many revolved around huge, strangely shaped silver balloons. Whatever else was going on, one thing was clear: this patch of desert had been chosen to act as a new interface between Earth and the heavens.

If anywhere, then, was ripe for alien sightings during the early days of the Cold War, it was this desolate corner of America. For would-be conspiracy theorists, the air of secrecy that hung over the valley was like oxygen. It made no difference that the military authorities insisted the anthropomorphic figures were simply parachute test dummies, ordered in bulk from the Sierra Engineering Company of California, and known generically by the thoroughly Earthly nickname of 'Sierra Sam'. To some, they were and always would be aliens who were the subjects of a cover-up.

Smashed mannequins were not the only unusual spectacle to be viewed by those with free access to the scrubby Tularosa Basin during the mid-fifties. Anyone in the right spot on 10 December 1954, for example, would have seen a rocket-powered sled streaking across the desert floor so fast that it left for dead the T-33 fighter tracking it from above. Within five seconds of its launch, the Sonic Wind, nine rocket jets bursting from its back, was hurtling down its track at 632 m.p.h., roughly the speed of a low-calibre rifle bullet. Then it slammed into a specially designed trough of water, sending a vast, smooth plume of liquid into the air. In less than one and a half seconds, it was brought to a complete halt. And all this with a short, middle-aged man strapped to its front.

Photographs taken of the test subject's face during this ordeal show it grotesquely distorted, as though all the bones had been taken out on a windy day. He had every reason to grimace: at the speed at which he was travelling, every grain of sand in the air was transformed into a vicious projectile capable of flying through his protective clothing with the ease of a needle. Then, at the moment of braking, he was subjected to a deceleration force more than forty times that of gravity. For an instant, his weight soared to almost four tons. The whole experience had been designed to mimic the effects of ejecting from an aircraft travelling at 1000 m.p.h. at 40,000 feet. Small wonder he clenched down on the bite plate with which he had been thoughtfully provided.

The man who willingly subjected himself to this torture was John Paul Stapp of the US Air Force Medical Corps. He was an unconventional medic who approached aviation medicine with the monomaniacal zeal of a missionary. Raised by strict Baptist parents in the forests of northern Brazil, as an adult Stapp had gradually sublimated the principles of his upbringing into a relentless war against the forces that threatened pilots in the air. His dedication was legendary. On one earlier test, Stapp had emerged from the rocket sled with bleeding eyes and covered with sandblast blisters only to learn that he had become the original victim of Murphy's Law. An unfortunate assistant of that name had found the one and only way to attach every single monitoring sensor to his body backwards. Stapp's suffering had therefore been in vain. His response was to hop on for another go.

This was not the first time that Stapp had made himself a living martyr to science. In the late 1940s, he had made repeated flights up to 47,000 feet in unheated and unpressurised aircraft to make a subjective study of the effects of the bends. He concluded that they were extremely unpleasant. When it came to learning about windblast, he had adopted a similarly direct approach, placing himself in the back seat of a Northrop F-89 with its canopy cut away while the pilot steered the plane into a 570 m.p.h. dive. Anyone who has leaned out of a car window at even an eighth of that speed will have some appreciation of this feat. Stapp's manifest preparedness to put his money where his mouth was instilled a powerful ethic in everyone who worked for him: never ask anyone to do what you wouldn't be prepared to do yourself.

Increasingly, what the authorities in the US Air Force were asking their pilots to do was to risk their lives at unprecedented speeds and altitudes. Ever since the end of the Second World War, it had been apparent that the battles of the future would be fought far above the arena of the Spitfire and the Messerschmitt. In October 1947, Chuck Yeager had broken the sound barrier in the orange firework that was the Bell X-1 rocket plane, shooting into the stratosphere with the feeling that he had burst through the roof of the sky. As aircraft technology continued its accelerating development, it was a certainty that others would follow him into that realm of perpetual night. In 1952, the powerful Aerodynamics Committee of the National Advisory Committee for Aeronautics formally resolved that NACA should intensify its research on flight at altitudes between twelve and fifty miles and at speeds of between 4 and 10 Mach (1 Mach is the speed of sound, which varies according to temperature and altitude, but which at 15°C/59°F at sea-level is approximately 760 m.p.h.). It further resolved to 'devote a modest effort to problems associated with unmanned and manned flight at altitudes from 50 miles to infinity and at speeds from Mach number 10 to the velocity of escape from the earth's gravity'. The scramble for space was now on in earnest.

Although it was a racing certainty that people would increasingly find themselves in the upper reaches of the atmosphere, nobody knew exactly how they would use this new theatre of activity, whether militarily or otherwise. What was clear, though, was that they would find themselves subject to risks and stresses, both physical and psychological, that no one had experienced before. Some of these dangers would come from the strange, frigid and airless environment to which they were heading, others from what it would take to get them there and back. There was a pressing need to establish the limits of human tolerance to the forces of acceleration and deceleration. And to answer the question of what to do when things went wrong up there.

Before the military authorities would sanction manned forays into the fringes of space, they had to be convinced that humans were capable of surviving the conditions they might expect to encounter there. They also needed to know that in the event of an emergency there was some chance of them escaping. This was not only a symptom of genuine compassion for Air Force personnel: space research was still widely believed to reside somewhere on the dotty fringes of science, and it was doubtful that the American public would tolerate the loss of many lives in pursuit of what it saw as pie in the-sky. There were also economic considerations. It took a long time and cost many thousands of dollars to train a top military pilot. Every effort must be made to safeguard that investment.

It was for this reason that the Holloman Air Force Base of the mid-1950s played host to parachuting robots and reverberated with the thunder of rocket-sled tests. Stapp and his colleagues at Holloman were doing everything they could to demonstrate the viability of bail-out at super-high speeds and altitudes, short of sending people up to experience it. But, sooner rather than later, they would exhaust the knowledge they could hope to acquire from earthbound simulations and experiments with dummies. Someone was going to have to go into the cruel environment of space to demonstrate that survival there was possible. And then someone would have to perform a successful bail-out from the other side of the atmosphere. In both endeavours, there would be a central role for the ginger-haired pilot who stared down from the cockpit of the T-33 that day, watching in wonder as his boss pulled away from him on a sled. His name was Joe Kittinger.

———

Wernher von Braun and his colleagues from Peenemunde were not the only German scientists with space on their minds harvested by the United States at the end of the war. One of the most prominent of the remainder was Hubertus Strughold. Often described as the 'father of space medicine', Strughold had an unparalleled knowledge of the effects of extremes of pressure and temperature on the human organism. The fact that, according to many, he had acquired it in the laboratories of Dachau was depressingly easy to overlook in the feeding frenzy for technological advantage.

In 1951, Strughold made a speech at a symposium of aviation-medicine experts in Texas that would have far-reaching consequences for the embryonic space effort. At the time, it was conventional within the scientific community to set the boundary between space and the atmosphere approximately 600 miles above the surface of the Earth. This might, Strughold argued, make sense in terms of the disciplines of physics and astronomy, but from the perspective of the biologist, it was far too high. As far as bio-function was concerned, the dwindling atmosphere started to take on the characteristics of space at an altitude as low as 50,000 feet. By 80,000 feet, this process was substantially complete. 'What we call upper atmosphere in the physical sense,' he declared, 'must be considered – in terms of biology – as space in its total form.' He named the region of atmospheric space equivalence that he had identified the 'aeropause'.

For men like John Paul Stapp, this was a realisation of immense significance. It meant that to demonstrate the possibility of successful human space travel, it was only necessary to send an aeronaut a fraction as high as had been previously supposed. Indeed, the lower regions of Strughold's 'aeropause' had already been penetrated many times. The problem was getting someone to stay there long enough for any useful conclusions to be drawn. Conventional aircraft could poke their noses into the stratosphere by virtue of momentum gained at lower altitudes, but were basically useless once they had run out of air to use for combustion. Ballistic missiles and rocket planes were able to generate their own oxygen for this purpose, but they, too, were only briefly in the air. They were also prohibitively expensive. This left only one affordable option with the necessary stamina: the balloon.

John Paul Stapp had first begun to consider the balloon as a means to further his researches in the early fifties, while stationed at Wright Field Air Force Base in Ohio. Balloon technology, he was aware, had advanced to the point where access to Strughold's 'aeropause' was now realistically achievable. Stapp's musings in this direction were given a considerable boost by his subsequent transfer to the Aeromedical Laboratory at Holloman. There, in addition to the V-2 tests, they had been conducting high-altitude balloon experiments for years.

The initial catalyst for balloon research at Holloman had come from the Japanese. In the latter days of the war, Japan released over 9000 incendiary balloons or 'Fugos' into the newly discovered jet stream, a rapid, easterly flowing river of air some six miles up in the sky. These hydrogen-filled rice-paper devices were intended to float all the way to the United States. In the event, over a thousand made it, some penetrating as far inland as Michigan and Texas. In May 1945, six curious picnickers were killed in Oregon by a balloon bomb that exploded as they dragged it from some woods. The US military woke up belatedly to the possibilities presented by aerostats, and decided to initiate balloon experiments of its own. Southern New Mexico, with its stable weather patterns, proved the ideal location.

Polyethylene had been discovered by accident in the early 1930s by the British firm ICI; it is now the most popular plastic in the world. This is the polymer that makes greenhouse films, heavy-duty rubbish bags, grocery bags, shampoo bottles, plastic pallets, toys, pipes, and even bulletproof vests. For such a versatile material, its structure is very simple: a long chain of carbon atoms, with two hydrogen atoms attached to each one. In 1946, the US Navy contracted the General Mills Corporation, the breakfast-cereals giant, to investigate the possibility of using polyethylene as a replacement for heavy rubber in the construction of balloon envelopes. The fall of the Malay peninsula to the Japanese had killed off the supply of natural rubber anyway, and the synthetic version, neoprene, had many drawbacks as a balloon material. Because it wasn't transparent, neoprene absorbed a considerable amount of heat from sunlight. This raised the temperature of the gas in the balloon, causing even more expansion than was inevitable due to the reduction in outside air pressure with increasing altitude. Something non-expanding and transparent was required, and polyethylene fitted the bill perfectly. Its adoption was a key development in balloon technology.

On 3 July 1947, Charlie Moore, a graduate student at New York University, launched the world's first experimental polyethylene balloon from Alamogordo Airfield. Moore's seminal work with high-altitude balloons became the basis of a US Air Force experimental research programme later dubbed 'Project Mogul'. High-altitude balloons (which floated at about 45,000 feet) equipped with ultra-sensitive microphones were used to detect and monitor the frequencies associated with nuclear-explosives testing. In both shape and scale, these were a long way from conventional balloons. Airline pilots, confronted by vast, silver exclamation marks in the sky, were unable to tell if they were one or fifty miles away. Predictably, the number of alien sightings began to multiply. Official government reports from the mid-1990s claim that the most celebrated, the so-called Roswell Incident, was simply the result of over-imaginative UFO fanatics conflating the evidence of debris from Mogul and the later parachute dummy tests. The spirit of Gonesse, it seemed, was alive and well.

After his stint at the New York University Graduate School, where he carried out balloon research for the US Army Air Force, Moore went to work for General Mills, which at the time was branching out into the meteorological ballooning business with its Aeronautical Research Laboratory. In 1949, while employed at General Mills, Moore made aviation history of sorts by becoming the first man to pilot a plastic balloon. From a field north of Minneapolis, he took the balloon up to 10,000 feet, attached to it by his parachute harness.

Other noteworthy post-war balloon projects included Project Moby Dick, in which 500 balloons were launched from a range of sites across the US, ostensibly to investigate stratospheric air currents, but actually to take aerial reconnaissance photographs of China and the USSR. Project Helios was a doomed attempt by the US Navy to send a man to 100,000 feet by means of a cluster of 100 helium balloons: the system proved impossible to launch in a controlled manner. But of all the balloon projects of the post-war era, the most relevant from John Paul Stapp's perspective were the ones investigating cosmic rays.

When the American military authorities began seriously to countenance sending men into space, one of their major concerns was how the human organism would be affected by cosmic rays. These mysterious phenomena had been discovered as far back as 1912, as scientists searched for an answer to the puzzling question of why the air in their electroscopes invariably became electrically charged, or 'ionised', no matter how well they insulated their equipment from possible causes. Because electroscopes were themselves designed to detect electrical charges, such as those generated by the recently discovered phenomenon of radiation, this ionisation appeared to interfere with their accuracy. Or would, until it was properly explained.

The general consensus was that the troublesome ionisation must be caused by radioactive minerals underground. To test this hypothesis, Victor Hess, an Austrian scientist, decided to take an electroscope up in a balloon. If the radioactive mineral theory was correct, the electroscope could be expected to register fewer 'hits' the higher the balloon rose above the surface of the Earth. Instead, to his considerable surprise, Hess found it registering more. The pattern continued all the way to his maximum altitude of 16,000 feet.

Evidently, the source of the radiation was in the sky. The

obvious culprit, the Sun, was virtually eliminated from the enquiry when Hess made another ascent during an eclipse, and found his electroscope clicking merrily away just the same. This suggested powerfully that the radiation originated in outer space. And because it was initially believed to be electromagnetic in nature, it was conceived of in terms of waves, hence the term 'cosmic ray'.

In the intervening four decades, surprisingly little progress had been made in the study of cosmic rays. The most significant discovery had been that they were not rays at all, but highly charged particles that zipped through the void at almost the speed of light. Research was hindered by the fact that the vast majority of cosmic rays were known to collide with gas molecules in the Earth's atmosphere, causing them to break up or slow down long before they could penetrate its lower regions (the atmosphere is now known to be roughly as effective a shield as a wall of concrete thirteen feet thick). There was, however, an up-side to this: were it not so, many argued that life on Earth would never have got started. Contrariwise, some scientists believed that genetic mutations caused by cosmic rays had been essential to the process of evolution.

Today we know that the majority of cosmic rays originate in supernovae, neutron stars, black holes, galactic nuclei and other celestial exotica. Most are atomic nuclei, stripped of their surrounding electrons by forces strong enough to blow stars to smithereens then accelerated to tremendous velocities. The most powerful that have been detected have had energies comparable to baseballs travelling at 100 m.p.h., despite being considerably smaller than atoms (typically 10^{-18} metres in radius). Fortunately such monsters are rare, with perhaps one falling on every square mile of the Earth's surface every year or so. We also know that the Sun's contribution to this radioactive bombardment, while usually fairly minimal, can rise by a factor of a million or more during exceptional solar storms. In the early 1950s, however, much of this remained to be learned.

The man at Holloman with the most expertise in the effects of cosmic rays on living tissues was David Simons (it was he, incidentally, who had performed the role of project surgeon for Stapp's Holloman rocket-sled tests). This tall, gaunt-faced scientist had been involved in the earliest animal experiments at White Sands, beginning in 1948 with the upwards despatch of a nine-pound Rhesus monkey named Albert inside the nose-cone of a modified V2. But the recovery rates were awful – it was three years before any live animals were retrieved – and the exposure to the space-equivalent environment was so brief that little of any use was learned by such experiments. Increasingly, therefore, Simons had turned his attention to balloons.

Right from the start, Simons' live balloon tests produced encouraging results. In the first flight, in February 1953, seven hamsters flew all the way to Florida from New Mexico at 90,000 feet and survived. (This feat was made even more impressive by the fact that the naval authorities who found their capsule *mailed* Holloman for instructions as to what to do with it. The pioneering rodents were therefore imprisoned for almost a week.) Over the next two years, Simons sent entire menageries of creatures into the ether, from cats and dogs to mould cultures and fruit-flies. His increasing conviction was that cosmic rays were relatively harmless. Their most troubling effect seemed to be a tendency to promote premature greying in black mice.

Other scientists, however, were not so sure. Among them was Dr Jacob Eugester, a Swiss scientist whose willingness to make himself the subject of alarming experiments was a match even for John Paul Stapp. Somehow, the eccentric Berne-based Eugester managed to secure a place in one of

Simons' balloon capsules for a payload of his own, consisting of a handful of oat seeds and some samples of his own dried skin. He later pronounced that the seeds had produced major mutations after just three generations, and that dark granules had appeared on the skin after he had grafted it back on to his body. Eugester was convinced that these marks corresponded to points where the samples had been struck by cosmic rays. Simons thought it more likely that they had something to do with the fact that the skin was already long dead when it was reimplanted. With this shadow cast over Eugester's choice of methodology, Simons felt reasonably secure in discounting his findings on the oats.

One August day in 1955, Stapp walked into Simons' office at Holloman Air Force Base and asked him if he fancied taking his cosmic-ray experiments to the next stage by following his animals twenty miles up into the sky himself. Simons was flabbergasted – he had always assumed that the honour would fall to one of the glamour-boy test pilots. It was not an offer he could turn down, either as a scientist or as a man of principle. John Paul Stapp had shown him the value of leading by example. If Simons was going to declare it safe up there, he had to be prepared to prove it in person.

It came as no surprise to David Simons to learn that Stapp wanted Joe Kittinger to train as an alternative pilot for the mission. The two men had met the previous year when Simons had needed a pilot to help him study the effects of weightlessness. He knew that the conditions of zero gravity could be duplicated in an aeroplane by flying it through certain precisely angled arcs. In essence, the process involved the plane being flown precisely enough to match the occupants' natural fall back to Earth. All that was needed was a sufficiently skilful pilot, and Simons knew by reputation that Kittinger was his man. When he met the heavily freckled southerner, Simons had been instantly impressed by his enthusiasm at the prospect of trying something new. As he noted drily, a flexible attitude towards novelty was a rarity among flying men.

Shortly thereafter, the pair spent an afternoon joyfully pulling parabolic arcs in an F-89 Scorpion. They enjoyed their hours in this ancestor of NASA's celebrated 'Vomit Comet' so much that they continued to the point where the plane started to run out of fuel. Kittinger radioed a request for permission to land, only for it to be denied on the grounds that to grant it would put him on a collision course with another plane. 'Thanks for the information,' Kittinger replied, matter-of-factly. 'I'm coming in.' Simons was amazed by his companion's calm under pressure. Afterwards, he studied him over coffee. There was no bragging, no compulsive itch to tell his friends that he had just been through a compound emergency. Kittinger's palms were as dry as a bone. His whole demeanour confirmed what Stapp had told him: Joe Kittinger was the best pilot he had ever seen.

Chapter Five

MAN HIGH

To be a test pilot in the 1950s was one of the sexiest jobs in the world. The flying profession still basked in the romantic glow of the aerial exploits of two world wars, but for the test pilot, the glamour was multiplied many times over by his privileged access to a thrilling new generation of aircraft. He – and at this stage in American history it invariably was a 'he' – stood at the forefront of science, but simultaneously embodied a series of timeless masculine ideals. He was a nine-to-five pioneer, a jet-age cowboy entrusted with bucking the most powerful broncos in history. And the work was inherently heroic. A test pilot routinely put his life on the line so that others might not have to, like the brave neighbourhood kid who tests the ice before his friends pile on to it.

In addition to a rare degree of flying talent, the job required lightning reflexes, a James Bond-like coolness of personality and a willingness to look death square in the eye. In return, the successful applicant got to play with some of the best toys on Earth. And lurking somewhere in the background was an unspoken recognition that it was men like this who would soon be knocking at the doors of space. For such as these, the sky was no longer the limit.

Joe Kittinger's background could scarcely have equipped him better for what lay ahead. He had been raised on the legend of his first trip in an aeroplane. At the age of two, he had accompanied his father, an office-equipment salesman from Orlando, on a flight in an old Ford Tin Goose. Kittinger Senior had watched with tender amusement as a look of wonder settled on the little boy's face. From that moment, his future career path was never in doubt. 'As far back as I can recall,' he would later acknowledge, 'there has always been a quiet but compelling longing that whispered urgently to me of flight . . . there was a wonderful mystery about it all; this I remember with tremendous clarity.'

As a child, Kittinger spent his every waking hour trying to unravel that mystery, to make it his own. He avidly attended air shows and idolised the leather-jacketed and begoggled pilots who took part in them. He read books on aviation from the moment he knew his ABC, and built and flew endless model planes from the roof of the porch at the family home. But if these were the chariots of his dreams, the vehicle that taught him the most about reality was an old, flat-bottomed houseboat called the *John Henry*.

With his father and his younger brother Jack, Kittinger spent long, idyllic days in this Huckleberry-Finnish craft, plying the St John's river and its environs. The *John Henry* was his passport to the primeval Florida swamplands. And it was in these wild surroundings that he first learned to master himself and his environment. From the age of about ten, when Kittinger Senior first sensed his son was ready for the responsibility, Joe was allowed out on the water alone with his brother. The two boys fished and shot, and marvelled at the local wildlife. Joe was fascinated by the birds: even at this age, he was unconsciously assessing their aerodynamic characteristics.

Long before the brothers were ever let loose unaccompanied, their father had taught them how to deal with bears, raccoons, and the snakes endemic to the swamps. But now that they had their freedom they upped the stakes dramatically by taking to bare-handed alligator-catching. Their system was as follows: Jack would steer the *John Henry* in front of a line of sunbathing 'gators, then start shouting, frantically wheeling his arms around, slapping the water with his oars and generally doing everything he could to catch their cold dinosaur eyes. Joe, meanwhile, would sneak round the back, settle on a suitable victim – maybe a two-footer – and pounce on it while it was busy watching the show. The keys to success were to be decisive and to grab the neck and the tail simultaneously. Anything less, and there'd be trouble.

There was something elemental in this ancient encounter between boy and reptile. Hunting a reptilian adversary put all that was fundamentally human to the test. It was instinct versus reason, force against cunning, old brain versus new. Evolution itself was on the line. And like St George with the dragon, Kittinger won every time. He grew in confidence, like the charismatic Southern Pentecostal who handles serpents to strengthen his faith, and the conviction formed inside him that he, too, might have the power to tame dragons.

For much of Kittinger's adolescence, his fascination with flying lay relatively dormant, as he busied himself with more immediate concerns. Then, in 1945, it was vigorously fanned back into life when an Army Air Forces gunner came to work for his father. This man, freshly returned from active service, was doubtless bursting for an audience to whom he could recount his wartime adventures, and his boss's seventeen-year-old son was more than eager to oblige. He even provided props in the shape of his old model aircraft. When the ex-gunner took advantage of a government grant to qualify as a flying instructor, Kittinger became one of his first pupils. And so it was that the childhood dream became a reality, in a little Piper Club with floats for water landings.

The final ingredient in Kittinger's extracurricular education was a spell as a professional speedboat racer. He had made his début as an amateur at the age of sixteen, entering and winning a twenty-five dollar race in an eight-foot duckboat. Then, in 1946, when he graduated from Bolles military high school in Jacksonville, his father rewarded him with the gift of an old mahogany hydroplane. Kittinger never won anything in this splendid machine, but he developed a taste for zipping around the local lakes doing aquatic wheelies. Unfortunately, the cost of competing grew prohibitive. If Kittinger wanted to carry on racing, he had to turn professional. Then, as was already becoming the pattern in his young life, serendipity intervened. A wealthy acquaintance who owned several boats asked Joe to be his race driver.

Kittinger proved an astonishingly successful competitor. During his two years on the circuit, he won the great majority of the events in which he took part and, unlike most of his opponents, never came close to crashing. He seemed to be more at one with his boat and its capabilities than the other drivers. He had instinctive 'feel', and he knew it. His confidence swelled. By the time he was ready to leave Florida to train as an aviation cadet, he felt he was omnipotent. Then, on his last day's racing, the invisible hand guiding his career produced a timely double wake-up call.

The first lesson Kittinger learned that day was the supreme importance of teamwork. As he was apparently coasting to victory in his first race, his engine began to shudder violently, then stalled. Snorting with frustration, Kittinger was forced to move out of the way to let his opponents pass. He returned, livid, to his pit crew for an inquisition. It emerged that a mechanic had inadvertently installed a non-racing spark plug, which had snapped at the crucial juncture. The moral of the incident was not lost on Kittinger. It didn't matter how brilliant a driver or pilot he might be: if somebody further down the chain messed up, his best efforts would amount to nothing. Henceforward he would make sure that if he had to place his life in others' hands, they would belong to people who knew what they were doing.

If there was any hint of self-righteousness in Kittinger's

response to the miscreant mechanic, he was brought quickly back down to Earth by what happened next. In his second race of the day, determined to compensate for the earlier débâcle, he took a turn too fast and was flipped over by a gust of wind. For the first and last time in his racing career, he was forced to 'drink water'. The humiliation stung to the core. The Kittinger who emerged from the lake was chastened but wiser. Never again would he overtax his equipment or consider himself too good to make a mistake.

In the spring of 1949, Kittinger reported for basic training at the Goodfellow Air Force Base, San Angelo, Texas. Initially he found the strict discipline hard to take, and for a while he lagged behind his contemporaries in the coursework. But in time he came to appreciate the rationale behind the disciplinary regime – that a person had to learn to take orders before they could responsibly dish them out – if not the experience. With the help of an inspirational flying instructor, he quickly made up ground in the classroom. In March 1950, he was awarded his wings.

Kittinger's first assignment as a second lieutenant was to the 526th Fighter Bomber Squadron at Neubiberg near Munich. There he flew the wonderful old F-47 Thunderbolt fighter before moving on to sleeker, quieter jets. He also acquired a wife, Pauline. Then, early in 1952, Kittinger got wind that there was a vacancy for a test pilot at a NATO base in Copenhagen. He leaped at the opportunity, but in this he wasn't alone. Two other pilots from his unit also coveted the job. In the end, the three men decided to let fate resolve the issue. Each picked one card from a pack, and Kittinger drew the winner.

Kittinger's role in Copenhagen was to vet new fighters before they were dispatched to the air forces of Denmark, Norway, Belgium and Holland. Now, for the first time in his career, the lives of other pilots would depend on his skill and judgement. It was a grave responsibility, but one to which Kittinger took with relish. He made some two hundred successful test flights in Denmark, and when he was done, he volunteered for more. In July 1953 he reported for duty at the Fighter Test Section of Holloman Air Force Base in New Mexico. During his five years there, he flew countless special test missions. He also negotiated more than twenty mid-air flame-outs, successfully restarting and landing his aircraft every time.

————

Colonel Stapp and David Simons, the newly appointed project director, applied to the Air Force for permission to give their project the title 'Daedalus', but found that the name was already taken. They therefore settled for the prosaic but descriptive title 'Man High'.

As it evolved, Man High came to be about much more than simply taking Simons' cosmic-radiation study to its next logical level. The project aimed to study the effects of prolonged exposure to Strughold's space-equivalent environment from a wide range of physiological and psychological angles. There was the question, for instance, of light: would a pilot of the future be able to see properly in naked light unfragmented by the atmosphere? With the X-15 rocket plane already in the early stages of development, this needed answering – and quickly.

On the psychological front, there were even more mysteries. How would the human mind cope with isolation of a categorically different kind from anything that could be experienced on the ground? Already some jet pilots had reported bizarre sensations of detachment during brief forays into the upper atmosphere, blissed-out feelings of release from Earthly bondage that were scarcely conducive to effective decision-making. How much more intense would these emotions be if the experience was stretched to several hours? Particularly with the pilot knowing he was unable to get down in a hurry even if he wanted to . . .

In view of the formidable mental and physical hazards the Man High pilots would face, not to mention the unfamiliar technical demands of high-altitude ballooning, Colonel Stapp devised a rigorous seventeen-month training programme. Three men would take part in it: Simons, Kittinger as the 'alternative' pilot, and, at Simons' insistence, a second scientist in case he was unable to make the trip in person. That this individual's identity remains hidden reflects the military's protective closing of ranks after what happened to him early in the training process.

In order to establish whether any of the candidates was fundamentally unsuited to the task ahead, Stapp decided to throw them in at the deep end with a twenty-four-hour claustrophobia test. This involved placing them, fully kitted-up, inside a simulated version of the tiny capsule that would be used for the flights. Confinement for a day in a metal can only three feet wide was not necessarily the worst part of the ordeal. In this case 'kitted up' meant wearing a figure-hugging partial-pressure suit. In the event of sudden decompression at extreme altitude, this excruciating garment was designed to inflate rapidly, thereby literally holding its occupant together. To work properly, it had be too small for comfort, i.e. marginally shorter from crotch to collar than the person who had to wear it. After a few hours, the discomfort could be dementing.

Simons was the first to endure the test. Although his dedication to the project gave him the will to see it through, he was particularly troubled by the lack of air circulation inside the pressure suit, and grew so hot that he was unable to concentrate on the reading material he had taken with him to while away the hours. Next up was Joe Kittinger, who had to suffer the indignity of being the guinea-pig for an artificial gas mixture designed to minimise the risk of fire. This contained a decent slug of the inert gas helium. Until he learned to compensate, Kittinger sounded like Mickey Mouse over the intercom. The technicians struggled to suppress their giggles.

Kittinger was no greater fan of the pressure suit than Simons had been, but he bore up stoically enough until, at his own request, the temperature inside the capsule was increased to 80°F/27°C. At this point, he became snappy and distinctly unhappy, but he soldiered on to the end of the test. The nameless alternative scientist did not fare so well. Although he emerged from the mocked-up capsule without reporting any untoward symptoms, over the next couple of days he passed out several times and manifested all the symptoms of combat fatigue. The puzzled Air Force medics at Holloman arranged for a second test, this time with the gondola's windows blacked out. They also deliberately placed the capsule where it would be caught by the late-afternoon desert sun, with the result that the temperature inside peaked at 94°F/34°C. When the scientist emerged, he was ghostly white and apparently in the throes of cardiovascular collapse. Yet he insisted he was fine. In his enthusiasm for the project and his desire not to lose face, it seemed he had gone into denial about the fact that he was, beneath the surface, acutely claustrophobic. Banished from his consciousness, the terror he would otherwise have felt had instead attacked his body. The list of potential pilots for the mission had been reduced to two.

For the next phase of their training, Simons and Kittinger travelled to Dayton, Ohio, to put in some time in the decompression chamber at the Wright Air Development Center. With this device, which could generate a near-vacuum when the air it contained was pumped out, it was possible accurately to duplicate conditions at 100,000 feet. Here, as Simons observed nervously, the pressure of the atmosphere would be rather less than it was on the surface of Mars. The purpose of these simulations was twofold: to test the resilience of the pressure suits (which would be worn throughout Man High as a precaution against sudden loss of pressure in the capsule) and to test the resilience of the men wearing them. This time everything went well.

It was an integral part of Colonel Stapp's air-safety credo to cater in advance for every eventuality. He therefore insisted that both prospective Man High pilots travel to El Centro in California to gain practical experience of the parachute with which they would be equipped during the mission. For Simons, this was a necessary evil, but for Kittinger, parachuting rapidly grew into something else. He had already made a couple of jumps earlier in 1956, shortly after his appointment as jet-flying safety officer and instructor in survival and bail-out techniques at Holloman. His initial motivation had been the simple avoidance of hypocrisy: a desire to have practised what it was his job to preach. But by the time he was due to leave El Centro, what was once a duty had been transformed into a pleasure. A few weeks later, he went back, voluntarily, to complete his basic training as a USAF paratrooper. To hurl himself from an aeroplane and control what happened next appealed to his inner alligator catcher.

The final ingredient in the Man High training programme was altogether different in tone, an exercise as delightfully tranquil as its predecessors had been stressful. This was where Kittinger and Simons learned the art of free-ballooning. Simons was quickly seduced, describing ballooning as 'one of the most delightful experiences man has yet devised'. Kittinger, accustomed as he was to higher-octane aerial pursuits, might be expected to have found it rather pedestrian, but he was not the stereotypical adrenalin junkie and he, too, was enchanted. At one stage, he found himself hanging motionless over a Minnesota town for several hours, gazing benignly at schoolchildren at play.

Often, the two trainees shared flying time to conserve precious helium. As they drifted low over farmland, they lazily smoked together (which they would not have got away with in the hydrogen era), and terrified the local chickens, who took the balloon for some nightmarish predator. During these carefree hours, Kittinger and Simons bonded together in a way they were never able to duplicate on the ground.

To meet Stapp's requirement that they obtain their civil balloon pilots' licences, both men had to log sixteen hours' flying time and execute the same number of take-offs and landings. (The fact that they were using gas balloons was not unusual – before 1960, when the American Ed Yost almost single-handedly revived the practice of hot-air ballooning, this was the standard technique.) This gave them plenty of time to acquaint themselves with the eccentricities of the vehicle, in particular its tendency to respond to pilot activity (such as valving gas to initiate descent, or dropping ballast to slow it) only after a significant delay. It was a case of acting now and finding out a few minutes later whether you had done the right thing. Then, to complicate matters further, there were the effects of solar heating to factor in. Sometimes the pull of the Sun as it expanded the gas in the envelope would defy all reasonable attempts to descend. Flying a balloon was usually delightful, but it could be like trying to ride a recalcitrant mule.

Although Simons and Kittinger logged some of their required flying hours at home in New Mexico, as the project progressed they found themselves spending more and more time further north, both in and above the city of Minneapolis. This was the home of Otto Winzen, the man who had won the contract to build the balloon and its capsule. Winzen was a character: a German immigrant, an enthusiastic collector of rare breeds of duck, geese and swan and the highly successful manufacturer of a plastic-coated cardboard container named the Fluid-pak, used commercially for storing milk. His real passion, however, was ballooning, and he had been making polyethylene balloons for the armed forces since shortly after the Second World War. The Man High pilots had a vested interest in working closely alongside him as the envelope and gondola (the balloon and the passenger car) took shape.

The capsule that emerged from the consultation process was a dome-topped aluminium affair with six small portholes. Before a man could be squeezed inside and dispatched to the stratosphere, the capsule had to be subjected to a stringent testing process. To vet the air-regeneration and cooling systems, it was sealed and filled with enough black mice and guinea-pigs to replicate a man's biomass. Then, in mid-December, similar quantities of rodents were poured in for a 'live test'. The outcome was both worrying and consoling: the envelope ruptured in the extreme cold above 50,000 feet, but it acted as an impromptu parachute and the animals survived.

As the day of reckoning approached, tensions built in the Man High camp that went beyond what might have been expected, given the perilous journey ahead. At the heart of the problem was money. This was not a well-financed project. The military hierarchy, in a condensed version of the mood of the nation, were going through a curious period of double think on the subject of space. Secretly, they were thrilled by the prospect, but this was not an emotion to which they were prepared to admit in public. No one wanted to stick their neck out and be laughed at, and no one wanted to be seen to sanction too enthusiastically so risky a venture. As a result, Man High was run on a shoestring budget, and even then it relied on some nifty accounting.

John Paul Stapp was aware of the parlous state of the operation's finances, but he was too experienced and safety-conscious to be satisfied by the animal experiments to date. He insisted on a manned test flight. Inevitably, in view of his professional background, Kittinger was assigned the job of pilot. Intellectually Simons, as project director, could appreciate the rationale behind Stapp's decision – after all, as the colonel had pointed out, all the animals had done was eat, breathe and shit, and a human pilot would be expected to do a great deal more than that. But emotionally he was gutted. Once again, the jocks were poised to get all the glory while the scientists lost out. And if anything were to go wrong during the test flight, Simons might never get to experience at first hand the environment he had been studying for his entire adult life.

As Simons saw it, the essence of the problem was that Kittinger was not particularly interested in the research side of the mission. Instead, he seemed to want to break new ground purely for the sake of doing so. Simons' disquiet manifested itself in a near-obsessive concern that Kittinger was showing an unhealthy interest in the possibility of bailing out at peak altitude, and might look for an excuse to do so during the test flight. (He wrote, a touch prematurely, that this would be madness: the shock of opening his parachute at, say, 20,000 feet 'probably would snap him in half'). And though he realised there might have been an element of paranoia here, subsequent events would show him not to have been so very wide of the mark.

For his part, Kittinger was far from happy with a provision allowing the ground crew to terminate the flight at any point at the push of a button, whereupon the capsule would detach from the envelope and slowly fall to earth supported by a cargo parachute. To his mind, this was like asking a test pilot to fly a jet knowing that he could be ejected at the whim of someone on the ground. The tension would be intolerable.

In view of the growing friction between the two men, Stapp called a meeting at which he laid down the law. Kittinger was only to consider leaving the gondola in the event of fire breaking out, and then only after first trying to put it out with the on-board extinguisher. Otherwise, if something went wrong, he was to put his faith in the cargo 'chute. In return, he had the colonel's word that only in an extreme emergency would he consider terminating the flight by remote control.

With relative peace now established, the launch was scheduled for 2 June 1957. As the day approached, Bernard 'Duke' Gildenberg, the project meteorologist, produced a weather forecast of unusual excellence. A decision was made to launch the balloon from a flat field near Fleming Airfield rather than from the mine pit at Crosby, Minnesota, where Winzen's firm usually carried out its tests. In such calm conditions, the mine's steep walls would not be needed as a windbreak.

At 1 a.m. on the day of the second, a fully kitted-up Joe Kittinger was slotted into the aluminium tube of the capsule in Winzen's factory, and sealed inside like some futuristic pharaoh. The gondola was then flooded with an artificial, low-nitrogen atmosphere (60 per cent oxygen, 20 per cent nitrogen, 20 per cent helium) as a precautionary measure against the bends. If there were to be a sudden loss of pressure while Kittinger was aloft, any nitrogen dissolved in his bloodstream would be rapidly liberated. It would then form itself into life-threatening bubbles, in a high-altitude version of the affliction suffered by divers who surface too quickly. Kittinger could minimise the risk by breathing denitrogenated air for several hours prior to take-off.

Once Kittinger was fully installed in the cramped pod that would be his home for untold hours, and which, although the thought could not be entertained, might turn out to be his coffin, the gondola was picked up by crane and deposited on the back of a waiting truck. It was then slowly driven the ten miles to the launch site, and at 4.30 a.m., Kittinger was deposited at the point from which he would leave the planet.

———

Helium is the second most abundant element in the universe. It comes into being whenever two atoms of hydrogen are crushed together in the process of nuclear fusion, the great engine that powers the stars. Yet, although it makes up about 23 per cent of the cosmos, helium is rare on our planet.

This odourless, colourless gas takes its name from Helios, the Greek god of the Sun. And remarkably, it was detected in the Sun – or, rather, its existence there was reliably inferred – long before it was shown to exist on Earth.

In 1868, two men, Pierre Janssen from France and Joseph Lockyer from England, both analysed light from the Sun using the new technique of spectroscopy. Both found a prominent band in the resulting 'breakdown' that corresponded to no substance known on Earth. Janssen thought it might be a new variety of sodium. Lockyer took a bolder approach, and declared the discovery of a new element. He named it helium, after the aforementioned solar deity.

For a generation it was assumed that helium was an exclusively extraterrestrial substance. Then, in 1895, Sir William Ramsey decided to heat a piece of obscure uranium ore called cleveite. It gave off an unfamiliar gas, which he promptly subjected to the spectroscope. Its fingerprint turned out to be a perfect match for Lockyer's original helium. At last man had his hands on some of the stuff.

It quickly transpired that although there was helium on

Earth, there was only as much as was produced as a by-product of radioactive decay, and even then for only as long as something kept it trapped beneath the ground. For helium, left to its own devices, seems anxious to return to its more natural celestial home. It is so light that it is resistant to the pull of gravity. Unless it is trapped or chemically bound, it simply diffuses out into space. In this sense, it is not quite of this world. Fortunately, significant quantities of helium had accumulated over the aeons in certain deposits of natural gas, presumably located above once-strong sources of radioactivity. Many were situated in the south and south-west of the United States.

It was not just because of its scarcity that helium quickly became a precious commodity. It was prized by scientists for several remarkable properties. These included the lowest condensation point of any substance, making it a perfect medium for the Frankensteinian practice of cryogenics, and a reluctance to dissolve in the blood which made it an ideal background gas for pressurised breathing systems such as those used in deep-sea diving. But perhaps the most useful characteristic of the newly discovered gas was its extreme lightness. It is this feature that lies behind the Mickey Mouse effect whereby the voice of a person inhaling helium rises several octaves. Surrounded by a lighter gas than usual, the vocal cords vibrate more quickly, thus increasing the pitch.

The scene that confronted Kittinger as he stared out through one of the gondola's tiny windows was pure science fiction. Under the glare of floodlights, technicians swarmed around up to their waists in ground fog. Then, reverentially, they began to unfurl the membrane-thin balloon envelope onto a protective canvas carpet hundreds of feet in length. One end was attached to the gondola, the other clamped into a mechanical launching arm that would restrain the envelope as it filled. A series of pipes connected it to two tanker trucks standing nearby. Then, with a ghostly whine, the valves were opened, and helium flowed into the balloon.

It seemed impossible that the small bubble of gas that formed near the launching arm would be enough to get the three-quarter-ton payload off the ground, never mind into the stratosphere. Yet if all went to plan, by the time the balloon reached peak altitude, that bubble would have swollen a hundredfold. With lift-off imminent, Simons asked Kittinger over the intercom how he felt. 'No sweat,' he replied. Then, at 6.23 a.m., an explosive trigger released the launching arm, and the bubble raced upwards, towing the lower portions of the envelope in its wake. The capsule was pulled along briefly on rollers until, in a seamless transfer of energy, lateral motion gave way to vertical, and it, too, was lifted off the ground. Joe Kittinger, sitting inside, felt no sensation of movement. Nevertheless, he could see in the capsule's rear-view mirror that the planet was starting to fall away from him. 'Goodbye, cruel world,' he quipped, as he rose.

Once he was airborne, Kittinger's first task was to re-tune his radio to VHF, the frequency through which he was to communicate with the ground during the flight. It became immediately apparent that something was wrong. Kittinger could hear his crew, but they could not hear him. For the remainder of the flight, he would have no alternative but to type his messages to the ground in Morse code. He hadn't used it since cadet school. Still, there was nothing like necessity for stimulating the memory. 'NO SWEAT,' he typed tentatively, repeating what was becoming a catchphrase. Back at Fleming Airfield, Simons, who was monitoring Kittinger's vital signs, was once again impressed by the man's calmness under pressure. The read-outs for his heartbeat and respiration at the moment he became aware of the radio failure showed barely a flicker.

Even without the radio problem, Kittinger would have had a burdensome workload. Now that he was restricted to communicating one letter at a time, he had little time to look out of the window. But as the balloon reached 45,000 feet, something happened to make him change his mind. Suddenly, out of nowhere, the envelope was snatched by a river of air travelling at 100 m.p.h. Kittinger knew that this was the maximum force it was built to withstand. He was unable to stop himself peering out of a porthole. For a few horrifying moments, he watched as the wind dragged the envelope into an almost horizontal position, hollowing out the surface as it pounded against it. All the while, the gondola jerked sickeningly. Then, as quickly as it had started, the bombardment subsided, and Man High passed above the reach of it or any other weather.

Any relief that Kittinger might have felt was quickly tempered by the realisation that something was wrong with the capsule's oxygen system. The pressure gauge told him that the gas was being consumed far more rapidly than should have been the case. However, for the time being, he decided to keep this information to himself. Although he knew that, strictly by the book, he ought to start descending immediately, he felt driven to continue to the target altitude of 96,000 feet. As a test pilot, it was ingrained in him to continue a mission until circumstances or his superiors unambiguously compelled him to abandon it. Too much was riding on the success of the ascent – too many good men had laboured long and put their reputations on the line – for Kittinger to allow himself to fail them now.

Publicly his bosses would have tut-tutted at his attitude. Privately they would have loved it. Fortified by Kittinger's determination, Man High rose onward, haemorrhaging oxygen, and leaving the ghosts of all the previous balloon altitude record holders far behind in its wake.

Shortly after eight in the morning, Kittinger reached his goal in the sky. Only one man, Captain Iven Kincheloe, had ever been higher, and then only for an instant. On 7 September 1956, Kincheloe had pointed his X-2 rocket plane to the heavens and fired it upwards to see how far it would go. Carried by its momentum way beyond the point at which its rocket engines ran out of fuel, the X-2 had reached the peak of its arc at an astonishing 126,200 feet. But Kincheloe's achievement had been like the leap of a salmon: a few short seconds in an unfamiliar element followed by a rapid return to the usual one. Kittinger, on the contrary, would be staying there for some time.

His first task on reaching peak altitude was to go through a checklist and relay his findings to the ground. This was a laborious process in Morse code, but the crew were satisfied with what they heard until Kittinger got to point seven: the status of the main oxygen tank. It was here that he dropped the bombshell. 'ITEM SEVEN . . . HALF . . . DOUBLE CHECKED . . . HALF FULL . . . WHAT GIVES?'

This news sent Ground Control into a frantic flurry of activity. Finally, the crew got back to him with a diagnosis that stretched even Murphy's Law: someone, it seemed, had installed the oxygen system backwards. What had been supposed to happen was this: if a sensor detected that the pressure inside the capsule had fallen below a level equivalent to atmospheric pressure at 26,000 feet, oxygen would be released to bring it back up again. Instead, the device was trying to keep the *stratosphere* at an equivalent pressure to 26,000 feet. This was a losing battle if ever there was one. The precious gas was pouring overboard, and only the bleed-off was reaching the gondola.

To arrest the problem before it got any worse, Kittinger was instructed to turn off the automatic oxygen converter and start pumping manually. At the point at which he did this, his oxygen tank was only a tenth full. This gave him three hours to get down.

He now had another ball to juggle with: in order to maintain adequate pressure in the gondola while conserving the dwindling supply of oxygen, he was committed to an endless cycle of pumping and monitoring. Whenever the internal pressure dropped to the equivalent of 30,000 feet (slightly higher than before because the cabin atmosphere was now pure oxygen), he was to pump oxygen until the gauge showed 28,000. Then he was to shut off the valve, wait until pressure was back down to 30,000 feet, and begin the process all over again. While keeping constantly in contact with the ground in rusty Morse code . . .

David Simons, poring over the monitors down below, was mighty impressed to see that the crisis had not caused so much as a flicker in Joe Kittinger's vital signs. He silently acknowledged to himself a sentiment shared by all the military men around him: thank God it was Kittinger and not he who was up there having to deal with all this.

Aloft in his metal womb, Kittinger was feeling acutely frustrated. Here he was, in a position to enjoy a view unparalleled in history, and he scarcely had a moment to look out of the window. Inwardly, he railed against the system that had denied him funding for a full altitude-chamber test of the kitted-out gondola. But Kittinger was a professional, and he got on with doing what he had to. He also contrived to catch the odd glimpse of the bizarre beauty that surrounded him.

From this great altitude, the landscape below seemed featureless and lifeless, although Kittinger recognised that the small puddle in the distance was actually Lake Michigan, some four hundred miles away. All the colour had been drained from the Earth by a shimmering, illuminated haze, which Kittinger was disappointed to find obscuring the crisp, curved horizon of his imagination. But he was more than compensated by what lay above.

Beyond the band of haze, the sky was a familiar colour up to about thirty degrees above the horizon. It then deepened into a blue that Kittinger described as 'utter and unbelievable . . . the bluest blue a mind can conceive'. Eventually, this too-blue blue darkened into an impossible colour, totally black, but blue at the same time, and simultaneously purple. Language was having a hard time keeping up.

Before completely immersing himself in the battery of tasks with which he was confronted, Kittinger carried out some hasty, naked-eye astronomical observations. This was something to which he had particularly looked forward prior to the flight. With less distorting atmosphere between him and the heavenly bodies than any previous observer, he had been expecting to see an unparalleled celestial display.

First, at the request of his friend Duke Gildenberg, he stared at the perimeter of the Moon, looking for a puff of smoke that would betray the impact of a meteor. (Gildenberg had reasoned that he might well see one, given the number of meteors known to reach the Earth's atmosphere and that the Moon lacked a veil of gases to burn up such visitors.) Next, he looked for the stars. But on both counts he was disappointed. The combined dazzle from the Sun and the gondola's interior lighting had left him unable to see a thing. He would leave the stratosphere feeling distinctly unfulfilled.

———

From the moment he had first become aware of the problem with the oxygen supply, Kittinger had known that he wouldn't be able to dawdle at peak altitude. Accordingly, he spent only a few moments at 96,000 feet before valving gas to begin his descent. Unfortunately, Colonel Stapp then decided to order him to start coming down. Kittinger's temper was already somewhat frayed by the oxygen and radio problems. Now he was being commanded to do something he was already doing, which came under the heading 'blindingly obvious'. He reacted by winding up his ground crew.

'COME AND GET ME,' he typed.

This remark caused consternation at Ground Control. What was going on here? Was Kittinger high on altitude? Was he looking for an excuse to parachute? Had he mentally cut the cord connecting himself to Earth? Stapp and Simons had heard pilots' reports that there were Sirens in the high atmosphere, voices that tried to lure them ever upwards to their deaths. Colonel Stapp, who in other circumstances was not beyond a quip himself, sent a curt reply: 'Captain Kittinger, I assume you are only joking. If not, I am ordering you to valve as instructed. Right now.'

Kittinger wrote later that 'The radio made it all too evident that the crew on the ground was becoming almost frantic.' If, indeed, he had only been joking, he had seriously misjudged their mood. They were worried about their man up there. And because phrases spelled out in dots and dashes lacked nuance of tone, they were a lot easier to misinterpret than the spoken word. For his part Kittinger, though, felt slighted by what he saw as lack of confidence in his abilities. Nevertheless, he went along with Stapp's demand.

'VALVING GAS,' he Morsed.

Helium balloons are incredibly sensitive instruments, and small changes in their gas content or the weight they carry can have powerful but strongly delayed effects. The tried and trusted method of descent, therefore, and the one that Kittinger was now following, was to valve gas for one minute, then wait for five to see the effect. In this instance, it didn't seem to be working.

Kittinger soon worked out that the cause of the problem was superheating. As the Sun climbed higher in the sky, it was heating the helium in the envelope – and therefore expanding it – faster than he could ditch it. Now he had yet another battle on his hands: to get Man High on the move again without over-compensating and precipitating an out-of-control descent.

Before the balloon started to go down, Kittinger noted that he had two-tenths of a litre of liquid oxygen left, about enough to fill a glass. If the worst came to the absolute worst, he had twenty minutes' worth of emergency oxygen to see him through a descent via the cargo parachute, but this would be tantamount to failure.

Kittinger now multi-tasked furiously to get the balloon safely down to Earth. Almost as an act of defiance, he also insisted on completing all the scientific requirements of the flight. For three hours, he manually regulated the cabin pressure, conducted visual observations of his surroundings, operated cameras both movie and still, scribbled copious notes and managed the descent of the superheating balloon, while all the time relaying messages down to Earth in Morse. It was an epic performance. At 20,000 feet, the oxygen gave out, but by this point he was safe. He even managed to execute a delicate landing, touching down in a shallow Minnesota creek.

The mission was heralded as a vindication of Stapp's decision to send a test pilot. The problem with the radio was traced to a tiny loose screw in the channel-selector button, and no one said much to the press about the oxygen trouble. Kittinger also pronounced the whole thing a great success, despite having come within minutes of death. Test flights were supposed to identify the flaws in a vehicle, and Man High I had done exactly that.

Joe Kittinger had successfully proved the system. Just.

Chapter Six

SIMONS

In David Simons' words, by the middle of June 1957, 'Man High was [a] dying tree, its trunk severed by the painful hurt of a budget cut.' After the oxygen fiasco during the first ascent, Colonel Stapp was not about to sanction another flight without a fully fledged dress rehearsal in an altitude chamber. But this would cost money, and the project was $14,000 short. Eventually, however, Otto Winzen's company came to the rescue, agreeing to put up the necessary cash. Such was the addictive nature of high-altitude ballooning. The gondola was taken to a simulated 85,000 feet in a decompression chamber at Wright Field, and launch was set for the middle of August.

On two occasions, preparations for Man High II were abandoned at the last minute due to unpropitious weather. Waitresses at the local diner grew accustomed to their gaunt new client who came in to eat steak but refused all offers of vegetable accompaniment. Simons was adhering to what was euphemistically described as a low-residue diet. He was going to be confined within a small capsule for at least twenty-four hours, and it was important to keep his bathroom requirements to a minimum.

In the course of this anticlimactic period, Simons' fingertips became sore from all the last-minute blood samples. These had to be taken before and after the flight to investigate his adrenal response to stress and to check for any increase in his white-blood-cell count due to cosmic rays. Then, on the eighteenth, in anticipation of the launch the next day, he was sedated in the afternoon for the third time in the past four days. It was vital that he be well rested for his forthcoming flight.

Late in the evening Simons was woken. First, a microphone was strapped to his chest to record his heart and breathing rates. Then several photographic plates were taped into place, precisely aligned with minute hatch-marks tattooed on his arms and torso. Every time one of these plates was struck by a cosmic ray, a tell-tale trace would be left behind. The hit marks could then be correlated with the exact points on Simons' skin where the particles had entered, and monitored, for years to come, to check for adverse effects.

At 10 p.m., Simons climbed into his seat in the framework of the gondola. Forty minutes later, he was dropped into the sheath of the capsule and sealed in. Then, like Kittinger, he was lifted on to a truck and driven to the launch site. This time, it was 140 miles away.

As the lorry trundled towards its destination, the mine pit at Crosby, Minnesota, with its 425-foot sides, Simons spent a sweaty, uncomfortable night constricted inside his pressure suit. Unknown to the major, while he sat stuffed in his tin can, Duke Gildenberg, the project meteorologist, was suffering from an agonising dilemma. He knew the parlous state of the project's finances. A third cancellation would probably be fatal. But although the weather forecast for the Minnesota area was perfect, a violent storm was developing over the south-western states, and it was impossible to rule out the possibility of its gatecrashing the party. Gildenberg was in a cleft stick. Strictly by the book, he knew he should cancel. All his instincts told him to err on the side of caution. Nevertheless, he knew enough about meteorology to realise they could be waiting for certain weather for all eternity. He also had complete confidence that in the unlikely event of the storm moving in, the balloon would be able to stay safely above it. With a sigh, Gildenberg gave the go-ahead.

At 9.22 a.m. on 19 August 1957, David Simons achieved his ambition to journey to the stratosphere. As he rose, he sent an ecstatic message to the designer of the balloon and capsule, operating his radio with a foot-pedal. 'Otto, it's wonderful . . . like rising on an endless elevator,' he gushed. He then immersed himself in the business of collecting data. First, he took readings of the oscillation patterns of the capsule, vital information for the building of a balloon-borne observatory planned for the study of Mars. Then he measured the brightness and colouration of the sky. Every 10,000 feet, he took recordings using both a movie camera and a specialised piece of equipment called a spot-photometer. The sky grew darker with every foot.

At 65,000 feet, Simons glanced into the split-view mirror and noticed that the balloon no longer fluttered with air-turbulence. By 82,000 feet, the gas in the envelope had expanded enough to transform it into a giant, transparent peeled orange, its segments defined by the pinching of seventy load-bearing fibreglass bands. It would double in volume again by the time it reached its maximum height.

By 11.40 a.m., *Man High II* was gently bobbing around at a ceiling of 101,500 feet, a mile higher than Kittinger's peak altitude of ten weeks before. Simons likened its movements to those of a basketball being dribbled in slow motion in an upside-down world. He stared from the capsule in wonder at the planet he had forsaken two and a quarter hours ago. The gentle curve of the Earth's edge confirmed that she was indeed a sphere, but paradoxically, this new perspective only served to emphasise her mind-boggling enormity. Then, as he looked up from the horizon, he saw it was surrounded by a halo of blue. With a start, he realised he was looking at the sky, only sideways on rather than from underneath.

Still more perplexing was what Simons could see at the edge of the visible atmosphere. On his lap, he had a chart featuring every shade of colour known to man. But the hue he was staring at through his porthole wasn't a match for any of them. Where the sky merged with the blackness of space, it was saturated with a deep-bluish purple, which he could only attempt to describe through poetry. It was, Simons would write, 'like a musical note which is beautifully vibrant but so high that it lies almost beyond the ear's ability to hear, leaving you certain of its brilliance but unsure whether you actually heard it or dreamed of its beauty'.

For the remainder of the day, Simons worked his way through the formidable 'to do list' he had compiled over the previous two years. During his planned twenty-four-hour stint in the stratosphere, he hoped to carry out a total of twenty-five biomedical, meteorological and astronomical experiments. But, unlike Kittinger, he would have plenty of time to observe and contemplate.

Sunset, when it eventually arrived, was an event of life-changing beauty. For over an hour, Simons stared hypnotised as a curtain of darkness was drawn across the sky by what appeared to be a giant, faded rainbow. Above this slowly rising line, where the Sun still cast its fading rays, a shifting palate of reds, pinks and yellows gradually gave way to a blue that again had him reaching for metaphors. 'It was as if someone had lifted a veil from an ordinary blue sky to leave it polished and bright and clean,' he wrote later.

Then the stars came out. Prior to nightfall Simons, like Kittinger before him, had been too dazzled by the unfiltered sunlight to see them. But now they came forth in their millions. In the absence of an appreciable intervening atmosphere, they burned with a steady light rather than their customary twinkle. And as the sky darkened, many gained colour, revealing themselves in vivid reds and blues. When

Venus set, Simons was briefly able to watch it through a double thickness of atmosphere. The planet flashed different colours like a disco light: red, then green, then yellow. There were many other marvels to behold. Simons could clearly see Marko's comet, its tail twice as long as when viewed from Earth. Towards the north, the sky was 'doing the damnedest things', flashing with green lights that turned out to be the aurora borealis. Then there was the Moon. To Simons' naked eye, it looked enormous, with the texture of a thin, gauzy cloud. But, bizarrely, it proved almost impossible to locate with the capsule telescope. Viewed straight on, the satellite was exceptionally bright, but in the absence of any significant atmosphere, it failed to light up the surrounding sky. For the same reason, the stars adjacent to the Moon, which would normally be drowned by its brightness, were undimmed by it. As he scanned the sky through the eyepiece, Simons was therefore denied a subtle visual cue that all Earthly astronomers take for granted.

When the setting Jupiter failed to produce the kind of display put on earlier by Venus, Simons checked whether the balloon was losing altitude. Sure enough, it was. A certain drop was inevitable after nightfall, with the gas in the envelope now deprived of the expanding effects of the Sun. Nevertheless, this seemed excessive. Then he realised what had happened. The storm front that had troubled Duke Gildenberg had started to move in underneath him. *Man High II* was now cut off from the heat radiated from the Earth's surface after dark. Ordinarily this would have buoyed her up, and consequently the effect had been factored into the altitude equations. Simons knew that the balloon would eventually level out, but the question was, when?

The storm itself was certainly spectacular. 'Like a flashing neon display,' Simons remembered later, 'the clouds were shot through with sporadic pulses of light that showed up a glorious pattern of puff and shadow.' It was also unnerving. There could be no question of coming down with such a weather system *in situ*, and there was no telling for how long it might be around. Simons also felt less than comfortable with a 300-foot radio antenna trailing down beneath him. He had seen lightning shoot horizontally out of clouds before. What was to stop it doing so vertically?

Despite the stressful circumstances, Simons, who had now been awake for well over twenty-four hours, eventually dozed off. He awoke in terror to a burst of light. His immediate assumption was that the gondola had been struck by lightning, but a thorough check revealed nothing. Then it happened again. Simons' nerves were now on a hair-trigger. The third time the gondola was illuminated by a sudden flash he worked out what was happening. Several hours earlier, condensation had caused short-circuiting in the wiring of an automatic camera that was set to photograph the instrument panel every five minutes. During the night, the electrics must have dried out, sparking the camera and its flashbulb back to life. With intense relief, Simons drifted back to sleep.

At 4.15 a.m., he woke with a stomach-wrenching jolt. The altimeter told him he was now at 68,000 feet – lower than he would have liked to be, for sure, but still presumably safely above the clouds. Then he looked out of the window, and was confronted by something that shouldn't have existed. Less than two miles away, a thunderhead loomed as high, if not higher, than *Man High II* itself. Simons reasoned that he had been awoken by the balloon catching in a downdraught of air from this monster.

It was no use the ground crew protesting that thunder-clouds were impossible above 55,000 feet (or 60,000 at the outside). Simons could almost reach out and touch one. He had to do something before he was sucked down into the storm. He therefore announced his intention to drop 100 pounds of ballast. Ground Control warned him that, in the extreme cold of the night-time stratosphere, the shock wave generated by this might rupture the fragile balloon. For Simons, in his current predicament, this seemed a risk worth taking. He pressed the switches to release the spare batteries that would constitute his ballast, and counted to eight. Four seconds for the shock to transmit itself to the envelope, and four for it to run back down to the gondola again. Right on cue, the capsule shook. The balloon had survived.

Although this was enough to lift the balloon several hundred feet, Simons prayed that the Sun would rise soon and heat the envelope enough to put some serious distance between himself and the storm. The sunrise, when it came, was preceded by a startling flash of green. This was caused by the atmosphere bending the green part of the spectrum of light from the soon-to-appear Sun more than any other of its constituent colours. Hence, green was the first colour to reach Simons' retina.

To his delight, as the rising Sun warmed the helium, *Man High II* started to climb. The experiences of the night before had wrought a profound change in its passenger. Ascending into the stratosphere now felt like going home: 'I felt as if I no longer belonged to the Earth on this morning,' Simons admitted later. 'My identity was with the darkness above . . . I was separated now, emotionally as well as physically, from the Earth.'

He was now irritated by any communication from Ground Control which threatened to interrupt his reverie. This was a classic symptom of Breakaway Syndrome, the condition he had virtually accused Joe Kittinger of suffering during Man High I. Perversely, another symptom of the syndrome was ignorance that it had taken hold.

By 8.30 a.m., Simons was back at an altitude of 91,000 feet. Gradually, the balloon floated over and then beyond the margin of the hitherto endless-seeming mass of cloud. As he caught his first glimpses of the face of the planet in several hours, Simons felt like a god. He dictated his emotions into a tape-recorder: 'This cloud layer which terminates as an overhanging shelf is so solid that it gives one a feeling of being in heaven, above the rest of the world, where you can look down over the edge and see the poor, faltering mortals.'

Although Simons was obviously exhausted and keen to come down, and although the storm front was slowly moving away, the ground crew wanted it further out of the picture before giving the order to descend. At 10.45, Colonel Stapp asked Simons for a respiration reading. The answer that came back was worrying in the extreme. Simons was breathing forty-four times a minute. Although he was a doctor, and therefore knew that this was three times the normal rate, the information he was relaying didn't appear to trouble him. He was immediately instructed to measure the carbon dioxide level inside the capsule. It stood at more than 4 per cent, well in excess of what was acceptable. At this concentration, the gas would inevitably affect Simons' ability to make decisions.

The ground team hypothesised that the chemicals which were supposed to break down CO_2 inside the gondola had cooled to the point of inactivity during the night. Immediately, they informed Simons that he was no longer in control of the flight. His role was henceforward to be restricted to carrying out instructions from below. First, he was ordered to commence descent. Then he was told to close his face mask and switch on the pressure-suit breathing system. His head cleared almost at once.

Getting down to Earth was a protracted ordeal. As Kittinger had discovered during the first Man High flight, when the Sun was shining in the upper atmosphere, it was by no means easy to persuade a gas balloon to descend. It was vital that Simons didn't overdo it, as the rate of descent could be expected to double on re-entering the troposphere. Eventually, however, after thirty-two hours aloft, he brought the balloon down in an alfalfa field in South Dakota. He was 405 miles from Crosby. Immediately, a support helicopter landed, and another needle was jammed into his thumb.

The press, on hearing Simons' description of the nocturnal display in the stratosphere, suggested that the lyrics of 'Twinkle, Twinkle, Little Star' needed to be changed. Colonel Stapp made a drier assessment of the mission. He simply concluded that 'Human performance in an environment equivalent to space is now known to be possible.'

———

After the triumph of Simons' journey, it emerged that the Man High project was well and truly bankrupt. It looked as though this was the end of the road. But then something happened to put space research right at the top of the agenda. On 4 October 1957, the Russians launched a small metal sphere into orbit. They called it *Sputnik*, or 'fellow-traveller'. Every ninety minutes, the 200-pound satellite orbited the globe, beeping contemptuously at the Americans as it went. For the first time ever, an object had gone up and not come down again, and the western world reeled in shock.

That night, Lyndon B. Johnson, the future President of the United States and the then leader of the majority party in the Senate, was presiding over a barbecue at his ranch in Texas when he heard the news on the radio. As was his custom, he took his guests on a midnight ramble to a nearby river, but his mind was on the heavens. 'Now, somehow, in some new way, the sky seemed almost alien,' he later recalled. America suddenly felt like a rabbit in a large open field.

Shortly afterwards, back on Capitol Hill, LBJ passed a

damning verdict on the Eisenhower administration for allowing the country to be upstaged by the Russians. 'The Roman
Empire controlled the world because it could build roads,'
he observed. 'Later, when men moved to the sea, the British
Empire was dominant because it had ships. Now the Com-
munists have established a foothold in outer space. It is
not very reassuring,' he added, with a sarcastic reference to
contemporary tastes, 'to be told that next year we will put
a "better" satellite into the air. Perhaps it will even have a
chrome trim and automatic windshield wipers.'

Suddenly, new momentum was injected into ballooning
and anything else that might help the US claw back the space
initiative. Finance was readily available, and space research
was at last able to haul itself out of the closet and into the
public eye. Man High had been saved by the Russians.

If the first two Man High flights had primarily been
about hardware, the third concentrated firmly on the mortal
components of a mission to the region of space-equivalence.
The stresses experienced by Kittinger and Simons during Man
High I and II had shown just how important the character
of a stratonaut could be to the outcome. As a result, in the
run-up to the third ascent, particular emphasis was placed on
the process of pilot selection. The procedure developed was
to form the basis of the system used in the following decade
to select astronauts to go to the Moon.

The relationship established between Ground Control and
pilot for Man High III was to prove equally influential.
The previous missions had highlighted the importance of
having a team of experts on hand to assume control of
a flight in the event of a pilot succumbing to Breakaway
Syndrome or some similar misfortune. Man High III provided
an opportunity to explore what was required of such a team,
both in terms of composition and *modus operandi*. During
the flight, the plan was to experiment with entirely absolving

the pilot of the burden of decision-making, reducing his role to relaying information and carrying out the instructions of the ground team.

The man on whom the selection panel settled for the mission, a twenty-six-year-old ceramics engineer named Clifton McClure, turned out to be a spectacular vindication of its methods. While enduring the long, cramped wait for take-off, McClure inadvertently released the emergency personal parachute that hung on the wall of the gondola. If the capsule had to be opened up now, the flight would have to be cancelled. Once, and only once in his life, McClure had watched an expert fold up a parachute. With the minimum of fuss, he now put what he had learned into practice. The launch was able to go ahead as planned, on the morning of 8 October 1958, this time from Holloman Air Force Base in New Mexico.

If McClure had demonstrated a cool head prior to take-off, he surpassed himself during the drama that followed. An important part of the pre-flight ritual was the placement of a cap of dry ice on the roof of the gondola to prevent overheating during the ascent. On this occasion, the chore had been overlooked, with consequences that would almost prove fatal. Without its ice cap, the metal capsule was transformed into a virtual oven, a situation compounded by the heat generated by McClure folding up his parachute. To make matters worse, the negligent party appears to have been David Simons.

At 24,000 feet, the temperature inside the gondola was already 89°F/31.6°C. When the balloon topped out at 99,700 feet, McClure reported that his own temperature was 101.4°F/38.5°C. When he started to valve gas to begin his hastily advanced descent, it had risen to 104.1°F/40°C. And by the time he was taken to hospital, having executed an accomplished landing, it stood at an astonishing 108.5°F/

42.5°C. Somehow McClure had managed to stay alert and efficient where anyone else would have been in a coma.

———

With Man High III, the programme came to a close, having succeeded in all its major objectives. The next time an American left the Earth in a capsule, he would be heading for space proper. NASA now took over as the focus of research funding. Joe Kittinger, meanwhile, turned his attention to other duties at Holloman. For the moment, his yearning to return to the stratosphere fell dormant. He would get his chance to go back there soon enough.

Chapter Seven

EXCELSIOR

Old pilots are not a group with whom one instinctively associates jewellery. Yet every now and then an ex-aviator turns up wearing a little gold brooch that looks like a maggot with ruby eyes. Its owner is a member of the Caterpillar Club.

According to legend, the first person to save himself by means of a fall-breaking device was the semi-mythical Emperor Shun, some forty-two centuries ago. Trapped in a granary tower ignited by his murderous father, the ingenious young Shun is said to have grabbed two large reed hats before leaping from the top of the building, which broke his fall sufficiently to allow him to escape.

When the proto-parachute makes its next appearance in recorded history, again in China in the early fourteenth century, it is not in the guise of a lifesaver but as a popular form of entertainment. Another enterprising emperor, Shi Huang Ti, is said to have amused himself repeatedly by leaping from the Great Wall of China suspended beneath a giant parasol. Meanwhile, umbrella-shaped fall-breakers were standard props for contemporary acrobats.

The first European references to the concept of the parachute appear in the sixteenth century. In 1514, Leonardo da Vinci made a sketch of a pyramidical device accompanied by a note which explained that 'If a man have a tent roof of caulked linen twelve *braccia* broad and twelve *braccia* high, he will be able to let himself fall from any great height without danger to himself'. (A *braccio* is an arm's length.)

In 1595, Fausto Veranzio, a Hungarian mathematician/ architect living in Venice, reached a similar conclusion. He produced a detailed engraving of what he called *Homo volans* ('flying man'), together with instructions. 'With a square canvas spread between four equal poles and having four cords attached to the four joints,' he wrote, 'a man could, without danger, throw himself from a tower or similar eminence. Even though there is no wind at the time, his weight will create the wind which inflates the canvas.'

Despite their visionary abilities, both da Vinci and Veranzio appear to have been strictly armchair parachutists. Leonardo, in particular, is no more likely to have built a working model of his parachute than he is to have constructed a helicopter or most of the other technological marvels he 'foresaw'. In Veranzio's case, the question is rather more open. But whether or not Veranzio ever managed to turn himself into *Homo volans*, it seems that it was exposure to Oriental acrobats that led directly to the first European parachutes.

In 1688, a Simon de la Loubère returned from a two-year stint as French ambassador to Siam, and settled down to write an account of his adventures. One section dealt with the strange case of 'A Tumbler Exceedingly Honoured by the King of Siam':

There died one, some years since, who leaped from the Hoop [unexplained], supporting himself only by two umbrellas, the hands of which were firmly fixed to his girdle. The wind carried him accidentally sometimes to the ground, sometimes into trees or houses, and sometimes into the river. He so exceedingly diverted the King of Siam that the Prince had made him a great lord; he had lodged him in the palace, and had given him a great title; or, as they say, a great name.

Almost a century later, fate conspired to place a volume of the writings of de la Loubère in the hands of a watchmaker named Louis Sebastian Lenormand. The tale of the ennobled tumbler inspired Lenormand to conduct experiments he hoped would lead to a device that might be used to escape burning buildings. The story had now come full circle: this was exactly where Emperor Shun had begun. Lenormand built a prototype, and used it successfully to drop several animals from the top of Montpellier Observatory. With amazing synchronicity, he did this in 1783, the year the balloon was born. He named his invention the 'parachute'.

Over the next few years, various individuals experimented with this new device. As usual, an array of hapless animals paved the way. Joseph Montgolfier, who was *au fait* with Lenormand's design, dropped one unfortunate sheep from the top of the Papal Palace at Avignon six times in succession. In 1793, Jean-Pierre Blanchard, of English Channel fame, was responsible for the first parachute demonstration in America, in which a dog, a cat and a squirrel were all sent down under the one canopy. The début of the first regular two-legged parachutist, however, did not take place until 1797, a full fourteen years after men had first taken to the air.

André-Jacques Garnerin was described by one contemporary as a 'small, peppery man with a spade beard and waxed moustaches'. Captured during the Austrian defeat of the French Revolutionary Army at Marchiennes, he had plenty of time to ponder the questions of aerial descent during the three years he subsequently spent imprisoned in Buda fortress in Hungary. After his release, Garnerin refused to relinquish his dream. His persistence culminated in a lucrative public demonstration in the Parc Monceau in Paris on 22 October 1797.

The parachute that Garnerin had constructed for the occasion was, according to most accounts, about twenty-three feet in diameter, with a long central support pole connecting it to the basket in which its user was to sit. The canopy was held open-mouthed by an eight-foot wooden hoop sewn into it a yard and a half from its apex. This primed parachute was in turn suspended from Garnerin's balloon in such a way that he could release it with the tug of a line.

At a height of approximately 2000 feet, Garnerin pulled the release line. Naturally, the parachute started to plunge earthwards. Meanwhile, the freed balloon, instantly deprived of more than two hundred pounds of ballast, shot up into the sky. These contrary motions fostered the illusion that the parachute was falling much faster than was actually the case. The sense of drama was then greatly multiplied when the sudden drop in air pressure around the balloon caused it to explode.

When the crowd turned its gaze back to the parachute, it became apparent that the device did work, but only after a fashion. It was breaking Garnerin's fall all right, but it was putting him through a terrible ordeal. As the canopy descended, it lurched violently, swinging the car beneath it like a pendulum. With every arc, Garnerin rose higher, sometimes even above the parachute itself. The audience was aghast. 'I have been told that all eyes were filled with tears and that women, equally adorable for their charms as for their sensitiveness, fell into a faint,' Garnerin later reported. But he landed safely in a vineyard, just as the Montgolfiers' balloon had at the end of its first public demonstration at Annonay.

Garnerin went on to make a handful of parachute descents, but each time, they ended the same way: with him being violently sick. If this mode of transport was ever going to catch on, someone was going to have to do something about the stability problem.

In 1804, Joseph Lalande, a prominent French astronomer, proposed a splendidly counter-intuitive solution to this difficulty. The oscillations that had plagued Garnerin, he argued, were caused by excessive air pressure in his parachute's canopy. This meant that, given the slightest opportunity, air would spill from a point at the periphery of the parachute, swinging it to one side. When it swung back again, air would escape from the opposite side, setting up an escalating cycle. Lalande suggested that the problem could be countered by cutting a small hole or vent in the apex of the canopy. This would reduce the pressure inside and better control the flow of air.

The adoption of Lalande's recommendation immediately improved parachute stability. But there were others who advocated a still more radical modification. Chief among them was Sir George Cayley, who wrote an article in 1810 claiming that 'the apex downward is the chief basis of stability in aerial navigation'. Cayley's theory powerfully influenced a young Irish watercolourist named Robert Cocking, who had been obsessed with the idea of developing a non-oscillating fall-breaker ever since he had witnessed Garnerin descending wildly during a demonstration in London in 1802.

After half a lifetime of conducting experiments with models, many of which he launched from the top of the Monument in London, Cocking was finally ready, in the summer of 1837, to unveil his extraordinary 'upside down' parachute. The framework of this inverted cone was built from three hoops of metal, the uppermost 107 feet in circumference and the lowermost a mere four, connected by ten wooden spars. A series of 'crown lines', extending from the perimeter of the largest hoop, enabled the device to be connected to the base of the balloon that would lift it up into the sky. Other lines, slung from the lowest hoop, connected it to a small passenger car. To cushion the landing, this was padded with inflated pigs' bladders.

Cocking's first challenge was to find a pilot willing and able to provide him with a suitable launch platform. The combined weight of parachutist and parachute would be almost 400 pounds. This left only one realistic candidate: Charles Green, owner of the giant balloon *Nassau*. Green agreed to Cocking's proposal, but only with the greatest reluctance, and then only when the parachute system was altered to absolve him from the responsibility of effecting the release. This would now be down to Cocking. It was further agreed that a tackle should be rigged up to allow Cocking to be hauled up into the balloon's gondola in the event of a last-minute change of heart.

On 24 July, the *Nassau* rose majestically from Vauxhall Gardens in south London, towing its curious cargo beneath it. Green was accompanied in the gondola by his friend Edward Spencer. When the balloon had reached a height of 5000 feet, Green shouted down to Cocking that, in view of the excessive ballast, this was as high as it was able to climb. He also asked him how he felt. 'I never felt more comfortable or more delighted in my life,' replied the sixty-one-year-old. 'Well, now I think I shall leave you,' he added, after a pause.

'I wish you a very good night and a safe descent if you are determined to make it and not use the tackle,' Green called out, his voice tinged with foreboding.

Cocking's answer betrayed his intention: 'Good night, Spencer, good night, Green,' he replied.

Green knew that at the moment of Cocking's departure, the greatly lightened *Nassau* would rocket skywards. To prevent themselves being asphyxiated by the consequent rush of hydrogen from the balloon's neck and escape valves, he and Spencer had equipped themselves with a 500-gallon bag of air. As the moment of release approached, the two men crouched in the gondola and inserted tubes from the airbag into their mouths. It was just as well. Over the next five minutes, 'amidst the howlings of a fearful hurricane', the balloon climbed more than 18,000 feet, spilling tens of thousands of cubic feet of hydrogen on to its terrified passengers, which temporarily blinded them.

Robert Cocking was not so lucky. His parachute began its descent successfully enough. Indeed, modern aerodynamics has confirmed that the principles of its construction were essentially sound. But it was not long before the inverted cone began, sickeningly, to collapse on itself. Cocking's weight had simply proved too much for it. Three hundred feet above the ground, the basket finally separated from the disintegrated canopy, and slammed into a field by the village of Lee Green. Cocking's body was taken to the nearby Tiger's Head Inn, whose unsentimental landlord charged visitors sixpence for a glimpse.

Accustomed as we are to look upon the parachute as a life-saver, it is easy to forget that, in its early days, it was considered anything but. For many, Cocking's death was final confirmation that parachuting was a dangerous and foolish activity. Well into the twentieth century, its reputation was similar to that enjoyed today by the practice of being fired out of a cannon. Amusing for the spectator, perhaps, but strictly for the professional stuntman. In 1892, the great balloonist Gaston Tissandier was still able to write that 'The parachute, which to this day has served no other purpose than that of a curious device for exhibitions, has no practical use for the aeronaut.'

But Tissandier was wrong. As early as 1808, a Pole named Jordaki Kuparento had saved his life by means of a home-made parachute when bailing out of a burning balloon over Warsaw. But although men had been in the market for a reliable fall-back ever since they first took to the sky, Kuparento's achievement was somehow relegated to the margins of aviation history. Perhaps there were just too many Icaruses for the one Daedalus.

The early days of powered flight did little to modify the

perception that parachuting was essentially a form of show-business. This certainly applied to Albert Berry's pioneering jump from an aircraft on 1 March 1912 over Kinloch Field in St Louis. He even had a trapeze bar. (As he jumped, there was a dramatic shower of newspaper, which had previously kept the folds of his parachute packed neatly apart.) When the First World War ended in 1918, the first global conflict to have been significantly fought in the sky, there were still many pilots who would rather go down with their aircraft than entrust their lives to a glorified sheet. The prevailing attitude had been well expressed in an article in *Flight* magazine in 1910: '. . . In our opinion, the aeroplane itself is inherently the safest form of parachute that the pilot or his passenger can have, and they had much better trust their lives to it than abandon their posts, and rely upon an apparatus that might quite easily fail them in an emergency.'

There were many reasons for this anti-parachute prejudice. In the first place, it was encouraged by the military authorities, who worried that if parachutes were provided, their pilots might be tempted to use them prematurely. This attitude was mirrored in shape if not in spirit by the almost knightly ethic of the First World War fighter pilot, to whom bailing out of a stricken aircraft smacked uncomfortably of cowardice. On a less idealistic level, it was also a consequence of the topography of the battlefield. No one could relish the thought of drifting down over no man's land, a sitting duck for enemy snipers in their trenches. Then there was the question of weight. A 'Guardian Angel' parachute, belatedly made available to British pilots, would reduce the maximum speed of a DH-4 aircraft by three m.p.h., and its climb rate by fifty feet per second. This marginal loss of performance could be the difference between life and death. Most pilots chose to do without.

All these factors weighed against the parachute in the

Woodcut illustrating the belief, prevalent prior to the seventeenth century, that the sky was a solid dome. Were it somehow to be penetrated, many believed that the 'machinery' driving the universe would be revealed.

Above: An early illustration of the principle behind the parachute, drawn by Fausto Veranzio in 1595.

Below left: André Jacques Garnerin descends over the Parc Monceau in Paris in a wildly oscillating parachute, 22 October 1797.

Below right: Henry Coxwell and James Glaisher in mortal peril above 30,000 feet during their epic ascent of 5 September 1862. In desperation, Coxwell attempts to open the gas release valve using his teeth.

Above: The ill-fated voyage of the *Zenith*, 15 April 1875.

Below: Gaston Tissandier gazes at his dead colleagues Sivel and Crocé-Spinelli amid the wreck of the *Zenith*. Note the unused pouches of oxygen-enriched air hanging above the corpses.

Above left: Auguste Piccard and his assistant Paul Kipfer pose in the makeshift 'helmets' they plan to wear for their 1931 assault on the stratosphere.

Above right: Piccard cuts a celebratory cake modelled on his balloon *FNRS* following her record breaking ascent to 51,000 feet on 27 May. *FNRS* featured the world's first sealed and pressurised gondola.

Below: *Explorer II* prior to its launch from the Stratobowl in South Dakota, 11 November 1935. The enormous helium-filled envelope had a capacity of 3.7 million cubic feet.

Above: A fully kitted-up Joe Kittinger prepares to depart the Earth in *Excelsior III*, 16 August 1960. Several layers of protective clothing plus other equipment have doubled his bodyweight to 300 pounds (136 kilograms).

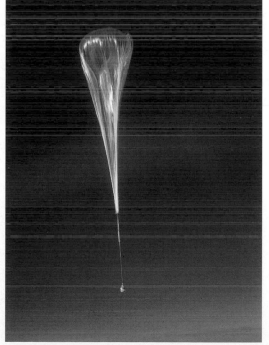

Below : *Excelsior III* photographed at 40,000 feet. The distance from the top of the clear polyethylene envelope to the gondola is 360 feet.

Kittinger steps out into the void, 102,800 feet above New Mexico.

minds of its potential adherents. But one in particular was connected to the then standard method of deployment. This was the static-line technique, in which the canopy was automatically released when a cord connecting the pilot to his former aircraft was pulled fully taut. This worked fine for the occupants of stationary observation balloons – indeed, several such lives were saved during the war. But for the pilot in a hurtling aircraft, the static-line method was a potential disaster. If, as was not unlikely, his damaged aircraft was to fall through the air alongside him, or if it was spinning at the moment of bail-out, the parachute would not deploy.

Late on in the war, the Germans had started to equip their pilots with parachutes, with some successful results, but before the Allies could respond in kind, hostilities ended. However, they had learned enough to appreciate the possibilities provided by the parachute, if only the deployment problem could be sorted out.

At the end of the war, the US Army asked the parachute unit at McCook Field, Dayton, Ohio, to develop a reliable parachute that would be amenable to mass production. The project was headed by Major Hoffman, but the key players were two civilian employees: Floyd Smith and Leslie Irvin. The static-line approach that had hitherto virtually monopolised parachuting was only tolerated because of the widespread belief that a falling pilot would be unable to control his limbs. Irvin doubted this, and proved his scepticism correct by successfully manually deploying the parachute a thousand feet above the ground while travelling at a speed of 100 m.p.h. He was so excited that he neglected his landing technique and fractured an ankle.

Three years later, Lieutenant Harold Harris bailed out of a crippled plane he was testing at McCook Field, and became the first man to save his life with the help of Irvin's device. The proud inventor promptly made a pledge to donate gold pins to any subsequent individuals who could prove that their lives had been saved, in genuine emergency conditions, by one of his parachutes (this criterion was later extended to include any parachute). The design of the pins would pay homage to the silkworm, which not only lowered itself by means of a silken thread, but also provided the raw material from which parachutes were made. 'Life depends on a silken thread,' was to be the Caterpillar Club's motto.

If Irvin had known what he was getting himself into, he might have thought again. By the end of the Second World War, the club already had 34,000 members. By the close of the century, the accumulated number of eligible individuals had passed the hundred thousand mark. One of them was Joe Kittinger.

———

On 19 September 1957, Kittinger, in the course of his routine work as a test pilot, was forced to bail out of a stricken bomber a mere 800 feet above the New Mexican desert. Shortly after take-off, his fourteen-ton F-100C Super Sabre experienced a hydraulic failure that made it impossible for him to retract the wheels. Next, a warning light flashed, informing him that the engine was overheating. Then, out of nowhere, the joystick shoved back his hand with a force he was powerless to resist. The nose of the bomber pitched sharply upwards, and resisted all attempts to bring it down again.

Suddenly Kittinger knew with great clarity that the plane was about to stall. He took a quick glance to check that it was not on a collision course with the nearby town of Alamogordo, and squeezed the handle to release the cockpit covering. As it blasted away, the helmet was torn from his head by a terrible wind. Then he hit the eject button. 'One swing and I hit the ground,' Kittinger would later recall. In the extremity of the situation, the physical trauma of the ejection failed to register with him. What was objectively a brutal battering was experienced as a blissful release. As the canopy of his parachute opened, he heard the roar of his abandoned aircraft. He watched in fascination as it dissolved into the earth, sending up a huge fireball. Then he hit the ground.

It was a suitably chastened Kittinger who, in April 1958, travelled to Ohio to take up a position in the Escape Section of the Wright Field Aeromedical Laboratory. No longer was the need for pilots to be provided with effective emergency escape systems just a powerfully held article of faith for him. It was now a matter of lived experience.

———

Of the many problems inherent in emergency escape from the new generation of jet planes, perhaps the most intractable concerned the mechanics of high-altitude bail-out. The upper atmosphere, it was known, was a merciless environment. Yet by the late 1950s, military aircraft were routinely climbing to seventy, eighty or even ninety thousand feet. It had been calculated that, in an emergency, it would take at least four minutes to fall from 100,000 feet to the maximum life-supporting altitude of approximately 20,000 feet. Could a man bail out at extreme altitude and survive the battery of hazards that would be flung at him? At the invitation of his old boss John Paul Stapp, Kittinger had travelled to Ohio to take part in a project intended to find out. It was named 'Excelsior', the Latin for 'ever higher'.

The problem of high-altitude bail-out was one of a conflict of interests. On the one hand, the stratosphere was emphatically not an environment in which you wanted to linger. It was airless and terrifyingly cold. It also permitted falling bodies to travel at far greater velocities than were possible in the thicker, lower regions of the atmosphere. Anyone unwise enough to pull the D-ring to open their parachute at such speeds risked tearing themselves and their equipment apart. On the other hand, it was scarcely a bowl of cherries to choose option B: to plunge through virtual space for an extended period at several hundred miles per hour. This was not just a matter of psychological trauma: the real danger was the tendency of the human body to spin.

The damned-if-you-do-and-damned-if-you-don't nature of the 'to pull or not to pull' debate had become apparent in the early 1920s. At the time, it was widely doubted that a parachute released above 20,000 feet would even open, while almost everyone assumed that a pilot who failed to pull his ripcord immediately on exiting his vehicle would be dead meat. There were others, however, pioneers like Leslie Irvin, who refused to take these presumptions on trust.

In the spring of 1924, Captain A. W. Stevens of the McCook Field Photographic Section addressed himself to the altitude question by leaping out of an aeroplane at 26,500 feet. He activated his parachute almost immediately, although not before registering that he was falling rather faster than usual. The parachute clutched manfully at the thin air, but there was simply not enough of it to inflate the canopy properly. As its edges alternately filled and emptied, the parachute pulsed spasmodically, like a travelling jellyfish. The unfortunate Stevens was jerked around like a rag doll. Already freezing, petrified and nauseous, he compounded his misery by allowing his oxygen bottle to slip through his fingers. His lungs were aflame as he gasped for air. Then a pocket of turbulence tossed him around some more. When he landed after twenty-five minutes of hell, Stevens was thoroughly clear on one point: it might be possible to open a parachute at great altitude, but it wasn't a very good idea.

The opposite problem, meanwhile, that of the falling body's

unfortunate tendency to spin like a sycamore seed, was identified almost as soon as anyone dared to attempt a free-fall.
Sergeant Randall Bose, in the early 1920s, was the first to
challenge the prevailing assumption that holding off from
pulling the ripcord for a while was tantamount to suicide.
In 1924, he made a jump over Mitchell Field on Long Island,
and allowed himself to drop 1500 feet before he opened his
parachute. A few days later, he tried to fall twice as far, but
as he plummeted, he began to rotate alarmingly; 1800 feet of
this was enough to convince him to abort.

What Bose was experiencing was flat spin, so called because
of the body's axis of rotation when in its grip. In a typical
flat spin, the aerodynamics of the human frame determine
that the unfortunate subject is flipped on their back, and
left staring helplessly upwards like an inverted turtle. They
then begin to revolve horizontally around a central point
an inch or two below the navel. Any rate of spin above six
revolutions per minute will eventually induce disorientation
and nausea. If the rate of spin grows high enough, to perhaps
one revolution per second, they will lose consciousness. If it
increases still further, to 140 r.p.m. or more, they may die.

In the light of Randall Bose's experiences, Major Hoffman
at McCook Field initiated a series of experiments to investigate the properties of the falling human body. At low
altitudes, it was discovered, a terminal velocity of around
118 m.p.h. would be reached after eight seconds. This seemed
to place a limit on the forces that needed to be overcome
to counter the risk of flat spin. Confidence was further
boosted in 1925, when Steven Budreau, an Army instructor
at Selfridge Field in Michigan, managed a free-fall of 3500
feet with no loss of control.

The success of the likes of Steven Budreau spawned a
rash of magnificent men in flying machines who astonished
jazz-age spectators with free-fall displays. From time to time,

however, one of these showmen would find themselves in an uncontrollable flat spin, with predictably distressing results.

As the years went by, free-fall enthusiasts gradually developed techniques to minimise if not overcome the risk of flat spin. The art of skydiving was pioneered by men like Arthur Starnes and Leo Valentin. It was realised that there was much that falling aeronauts could do to help themselves. If they found themselves going into a flat spin, the best policy was to drop the arm and leg on the leading side of the body. By altering their aerodynamic profile, this technique stood a good chance of pulling them out of the spin. They were also well advised to try to sit upright, thus counteracting the turtle tendency. Should all else fail, they could resort to drawing themselves into a tight ball before flinging out their limbs in a sudden star jump to try to arrest the rotation. But as planes started to go higher, it became obvious that these skills would not always be enough.

Project High Dive was initiated in 1954 to address the problems of high-altitude bail-out. Research on subscale dummies in the UK had revealed that spinning was the biggest problem associated with high-altitude escape. Four options for countering this tendency were explored: the use of skydiving techniques (rejected on the grounds that pilots forced to eject in the stratosphere were unlikely to be in a fit state to employ them), stabilising the pilot's seat with a parachute (this was found to prevent tumbling but not spinning), stabilising the seat with fins (which prevented pitch and yaw but not roll, and two out of three wasn't enough), and stabilising the pilot himself. The latter involved the deployment of a small 'drogue' parachute, perhaps six feet in diameter, designed to exert enough drag to make the individual fall in a stable, feet-downward position, but not enough to significantly impede his rate of descent. Kittinger, as project officer for Excelsior, believed that this approach was the way forward.

In the course of Project High Dive, thirty-five dummy jumps had been made from planes flying over New Mexico at between 25,000 and 35,000 feet. The dummies had been found to spin at anything up to two hundred times per minute. Next had come twenty-one balloon drops at altitudes up to 91,000 feet, with similar rates of spin being recorded. Then more plane drops with a new experimental stabilisation parachute, and finally another series of balloon tests from 68,000 to 102,000 feet. The parachutes had normally deployed successfully in these tests, in which the dummies had dropped straight down, but everyone realised that this was an unlikely scenario in a real-life emergency. The system had therefore been modified to ensure that the dummies tumbled in a lifelike manner after they were cut loose. At this point, the success rate had plunged to a dismal 50 per cent.

In 1957, High Dive was dissolved, its participants frustrated by their failure to find an answer to the flat spin dilemma. Project Excelsior was left to pick up the baton.

The first thing that Joe Kittinger did on his arrival at Wright Field was to settle down with the resident parachute expert, Francis Beaupre, to analyse the data accumulated during Project High Dive. Beaupre was a somewhat maverick escape-system designer who, despite his civilian status, had been continually employed at Wright Airfield since 1947. The feature that marked him out from most boffins was an unusual degree of empathy with pilots. This came naturally to a man with extensive experience of packing then testing his own designs.

As the pair sifted through the High Dive information, they noticed that something critical had been missed by their predecessors. Flat spin did not seem to kick in until a falling body was on the verge of reaching its terminal velocity. Up to that point, it was inhibited by sheer acceleration. More importantly, this meant that there was a window of several seconds' duration between bail-out and the moment where activation of the troublesome drogue 'chute became a necessity. The faster the subject could get away with travelling at this juncture, the better the chances of a clean and successful deployment.

The problem with High Dive, it transpired, had been that the dummies had not been travelling fast enough when their drogue 'chutes had opened to provide a sufficient airflow to inflate them properly. The process had taken too long, and while it was happening, the tumbling dummies had had time to garrotte themselves on the shroud lines. It started to dawn on Kittinger and Beaupre that twenty miles up, there would be no need to call the drogue into play for maybe sixteen or eighteen seconds. By that stage, the pilot should be travelling as fast as a jumbo jet. If this didn't provide enough drag, nothing would.

The brainchild of these ruminations was the prototype Beaupre Multi-Stage Parachute, or BMSP. It worked as follows. At a predetermined interval after the initial jump, a timer would release an eighteen-inch pilot 'chute. This would then fill and pull out the six-feet stabilisation 'chute. As this drogue 'chute deployed, it would pull out three-quarters of the main canopy, priming it for its eventual deployment. The remaining part of the main 'chute would be retained inside the parachutist's backpack until restraining bands connected to his shoulder straps were automatically released at a second predetermined height, somewhere in the biosphere (in other words, below 20,000 feet).

The next question was how to get a man to 100,000 feet. Clearly, the answer was a balloon, but what kind of balloon? The big cheeses in Washington were none too crazy about Project Excelsior. After his Man High exploits, Kittinger was a national hero, and no one wanted the responsibility of sending such a man on a life-threatening mission. The project therefore had to be run on a shoestring budget. It was for this reason that the ostensibly strange decision was made to conduct the tests from an open gondola. Not only would such a device be light, went the thinking, it would also be cheap to build.

If Man High had been the high-altitude equivalent of going to the bottom of the ocean in a submarine, Excelsior would be like going there without one. The fact that Joe Kittinger was about to head off for space in an open-sided teepee put a severe onus on his safety equipment. His personal breathing equipment, for instance, would not be a back-up as in Man High, but right there on the front line. Similarly, if he couldn't get the necessary pressure to maintain his metabolic processes from his vehicle, he would have to get it from his clothing. It was therefore a particularly meaningful gesture when Kittinger elected to make his ascent in the regular partial-pressure suit issued to Air Force jet pilots. This demonstration of faith in his equipment and solidarity with his brothers in the air was difficult to ignore.

The man entrusted with the task of vetting the clothing for the ascent was Sergeant Robert Daniels. This was a heavy responsibility. Kittinger would be exposed to an environment more than twice as high as anyone had ventured without the protection of an airtight metal shell. In the vacuum of the stratosphere, the slightest weakness would be found out. So, for the next few weeks, Robert Daniels was effectively Kittinger's guardian angel. Everywhere Joe Kittinger was heading, Daniels went in simulation over and over again.

During one ascent to 86,000 feet, the mounting of a restraining cable that kept Daniels' helmet attached to his pressure suit snapped. Immediately, the helmet shot upwards like a champagne cork. The vacuum sucked the air from his lungs in an instant. Daniels would liken the experience to having a black cloth rammed viciously over his face. Only the quick action of a lab technician saved him. But within days he was back on the job.

Daniels was not the only person to suffer during the pressure-suit tests. George Post, the alternative pilot for Excelsior, had a faceplate explode on him at a simulated 78,000 feet. The shock to his eardrums sidelined him for a month. Kittinger also had a Daniels-like experience at 100,000 feet, when he found his helmet riding twelve inches up his less-than-a-foot-long neck.

In late October 1958, initial BMSP test jumps were made from a Hercules travelling at 30,000 feet. Kittinger pronounced himself more than satisfied. The next stage was a live test from the lower reaches of the stratosphere.

If a hammy film director had been asked to imagine the ideal location for the launch of *Excelsior I*, he couldn't have done much better than the reality. Truth or Consequences was an unlikely place for such an ominous name, a little spa resort town close to an ancient lava flow. In fact, the place had been named after an old television show.*

T or C was also extremely cold in the New Mexico desert on the night of 16 November 1958. Getting Kittinger ready for the ascent was a major undertaking. First, a nylon belt containing the electrodes that would monitor his pulse and breathing was fastened around his chest. Next came two layers of underwear, the first waffle-woven for maximum insulation, the second made of heavy cotton. Above this was the partial-pressure suit. This was a close-fitting garment of

* In 1950, the residents of the settlement then known as Palomas Hot Springs voted to change the name of the town to Truth or Consequences, the title of a popular game show, on condition the show's host Ralph Edwards promised to attend the local annual fair for the remainder of his life.

elasticated nylon and cotton that covered Kittinger's entire body from the ankles to the neck and wrists. A network of inflatable tubes called capstans was attached to the basic structure, which, when inflated, would tighten the suit's grip on the body through the action of cross tapes. This would turn breathing into something of an ordeal, but at least, by maintaining the pressure of the air in his lungs, it would keep the pilot alive. Finally, Kittinger donned a quilted twin set and a blue winter flying suit. He now resembled the Michelin Man.

Kittinger's feet were protected by no less than four pairs of socks. These were, moving outwards, thin cotton ones, special pressure ones, electrically heated ones, and finally thick woollen ones. But his hands, because he would need to perform a variety of manual tasks while aloft, had to make do with just three protective layers. Last, the 'horse collar' was looped over his head, a rubber garment designed to form an airtight seal between his helmet and the pressure suit. Throughout the robing process, Kittinger wisecracked with his colleagues, psyching himself up and putting them at their ease. It was a performance worthy of Muhammad Ali.

The launch, when it eventually arrived, went smoothly. Throughout the ascent, Kittinger reported almost no sensation of movement. Hundreds of feet above him, the growing bubble of helium surged remorselessly but steadily upwards, a slave to mathematical forces. The gondola rotated slowly as it trailed in its wake. For its occupant, this was a nightmare. Once every revolution, the rising Sun streamed in through the opening, blinding Kittinger every time. As it rose, and the filtering shield of the atmosphere diminished, the problem grew steadily worse.

Frustration turned to alarm when Kittinger's faceplate steamed up as though it had been placed in front of a kettle. He was now effectively flying blind. But this dilemma was as nothing compared to the sickening realisation, at 58,000 feet, that his helmet had started to inch up his neck. With a shudder, his mind flashed back to the Daniels incident and his own horrifying experience in a chamber simulation to 100,000 feet.

Fortunately, an engineer, mindful of problems in the past, had tied several lengths of parachute cord from Kittinger's helmet to points on his parachute harness, so after it had risen a couple of inches, the torture came to a halt. Nevertheless, the experience left Kittinger bracing himself in anticipation of a renewal.

Next, Kittinger noticed through a small window in the mist that the needle of the altimeter had climbed beyond 65,000 feet. Amid all the drama of the last few minutes, he had overshot his planned exit point. He valved some helium to try to bring the balloon to a halt, but the ascent continued regardless. Not for the first time, the Sun was expanding the gas in the envelope faster than Kittinger could release it.

At this point, a lesser man would have burst into tears. Blinded, terrorized by the helmet problem and shackled to a vehicle he was powerless to stop, Kittinger was fast running out of options. He felt his confidence shrink and his temper shorten dangerously.

Then a miracle happened. Kittinger's faceplate cleared, instantly and inexplicably. He had his eyes back. (The team would later attribute this to the rising temperature above 60,000 feet.) At this point he was roughly an Everest higher than anyone had previously been in an open gondola. He had no time to waste. He pushed aside his concerns about his helmet, and began to disconnect himself from his vehicle. Then he ditched the radio antenna to ensure that the gondola would land safely when it descended, which it was programmed to do via its own parachute shortly after Kittinger abandoned it. Next, he moved to pull himself up. The first attempt ended in failure. He was fixed to the spot. His instrument pack appeared to have got wedged into his Styrofoam seat. At the third try he managed to wrench himself free.

The real problems began, however, when he tried to pull the lanyard that was to activate the timers for his parachutes. This piece of machinery was designed to pull out two knobs. The first activated the timer for the pilot 'chute while the second would arm the pressure-sensitive trigger that was to open the main canopy at 18,000 feet. On Kittinger's first tug at the lanyard, nothing seemed to happen. In fact, without his knowledge, he had set in motion the sixteen-second countdown to the opening of the stabilisation 'chute. Henceforward, everything would be out of synch.

At the third time of asking, the lanyard shifted. Kittinger jumped. When he stepped out of the gondola, for an indeterminate period he had no sense of time, no sense of motion, no sense of anything. The first 'event' was a vibration in his back as the timer for the stabilisation 'chute whirred into action. Because he had been in that strange, timeless state, Kittinger had no idea of how long he'd been falling. He tensed in expectation of a slight jolt to accompany the deployment of the drogue 'chute, but nothing happened. Suddenly he was struck by the appalling thought that it might have become fouled around his body. The image of test dummies spinning down to Earth in a similar predicament flashed through his mind.

While falling at over 400 m.p.h., Kittinger started to frisk himself in a panic, like a man desperately looking for his keys in a thunderstorm. He was unaware that the pilot 'chute for the stabilisation 'chute had opened a mere two and a half seconds after he had left the gondola. At this stage, he had been travelling nowhere near fast enough for the pilot 'chute to inflate. Without him knowing anything about it, the shroud lines had passed through his legs and wrapped around his neck.

Kittinger found himself beginning to roll over, until he was falling on his back. When he found himself going into a gentle spin, he discovered he could instantly arrest it by dropping his leading limbs. Then, just as he was starting to entertain the idea that he might be able to get all the way down to 20,000 feet in this manner, he whirled into a vicious flat spin. As had been drilled into him in his training, he attempted to stop it by first pulling in his limbs (which temporarily increased the spin) then flinging them out again. It was futile. He became aware of a sinister swishing sound, like the noise a car makes when racing past a line of lamp-posts.

What Kittinger was going through was a graphic illustration of why a device like the BMSP was needed in the first place. As he spun like a propeller, blood began to pool in his extremities, and his heart was no longer able to pump enough of it to the lungs to be refreshed with oxygen. His vision started to turn red at the periphery, then unconsciousness set in.

When Kittinger came to, he was lying on the desert floor with something wrapped tightly round his neck. It seemed almost beyond luck that he was still alive.

The cameras attached to Kittinger's body enabled the crew to reconstruct in detail what had happened to him on the way down. His maximum rate of spin had been eighty revolutions per minute. At 18,000 feet, his main canopy had opened and snarled around his spinning body. Seven thousand feet later, the pilot 'chute for the reserve had automatically released, and itself become entangled in the fouled main 'chute. This made it impossible for the back-up canopy to deploy. Kittinger would have been a dead man, had not Beaupre, in a supreme moment of foresight, catered for exactly the sequence of events that had unfolded. He had made the shroud lines of the pilot 'chute for the reserve deliberately weak so that they would snap once it had done its work. This had duly happened at 6000 feet, freeing the reserve 'chute, and thus saving Kittinger's life.

The Air Force saw no need to divulge any of this to the press. Excelsior I was proclaimed a great success. Meanwhile, improvements were made in preparation for the second jump. The helmet straps were strengthened, the heating system for the face mask was revamped, and the system for activating the timers for the opening of the parachutes was simplified. Now Kittinger would arm the timer for the main canopy on the way up, as soon as the outside pressure had fallen safely below the level that would trigger it. This left just one knob to be pulled out by the troublesome lanyard. The system was rejigged and tested hundreds of times to make quite sure that it worked every time.

On 11 December 1959, everything came together in Excelsior II: 74,700 feet above the Tularosa Basin, Kittinger pulled the timer knob, which popped out exactly as it was supposed to. The pilot 'chute opened bang on cue fourteen seconds thereafter, and from then on the BMSP worked like a dream. When Kittinger landed, he was ecstatic. Now it was time for the big one.

Chapter Eight

AIR

The White Sands missile range was a particularly appropriate departure point for a mission heading to the other side of the sky, for the geological feature that gives the site its name is as other-worldly as anything on the planet. Comprised of gypsum deposits washed down from the San Andres Mountains into a natural basin that allows them no way out, White Sands National Monument seems at first glance to be oxymoronic, impossible. This sensation can persist for quite some time. It looks and feels almost exactly like snow, despite summer temperatures well in excess of 100°F/38°C. It is only when you catch sight of the occasional yucca plant rising defiantly from this most unpromising substrate that you remember where you are. Nevertheless, driving into the dunes of White Sands remains a little like stumbling across a stray piece of the Moon on Earth.

There was also a less symbolic role planned for this 270-square-mile patch of glistening gypsum sand in the unfolding drama of Excelsior III. All being well, it would serve as a welcome and familiar reference point for Joe Kittinger up in the sky.

The launch site for the third jump in the series was situated a few miles from the White Sands, just the other side of Highway 94. In the small hours of 16 August 1960, Kittinger and Beaupre ate a ritual breakfast at a local diner, even though it was not yet two in the morning. Although he had been on a strict low-residue diet of meat and potatoes for days, Kittinger allowed himself to indulge in some strawberry shortcake.

Beaupre paid the bill – the captain liked to be in debt when he jumped. Then the two men drove off for their rendezvous with the balloon.

At 3 a.m., Kittinger climbed into the air-conditioned trailer that would serve as his dressing room. Immediately, an oxygen mask was slipped over his nose and mouth, and the process of removing the nitrogen from his blood began. Then his colleagues began to dress him. As soon as they had pulled on his first layer of underwear, there was a loud report, and the AC unit droned to a halt. This was a disaster. If the temperature in the trailer was allowed to rise to the level of the surrounding desert, Kittinger would start to sweat. Moisture in the clothing was not good news at $-100°F/-73°C$. He had even been prevented from dressing himself out of fear that he might perspire.

For a few worrying moments, the mission was in serious jeopardy. Then, with a whine, the unit started to blow cold air again. The dressing committee remained unaware that the situation had been salvaged by a sharp-eyed sergeant named Gene Fowler. When he had heard the air-conditioning unit misfire, Fowler had run to inspect it and realised that an earth wire had become separated from a key component. For the next two hours, he held the wire in place with his bare hands, struggling manfully to ignore the cramp.

Forty-five minutes before take-off, Kittinger waddled out of the trailer and towards the waiting gondola, still wearing the oxygen mask to keep nitrogen out of his bloodstream. He noted with satisfaction that a cardboard licence plate with which he had been solemnly presented by his five-year-old son had been stuck to the outside of the craft as he had instructed. There was one more legend attached to the *Excelsior* gondola. It read simply, 'This is the highest step in the world.'

Beaupre and Sergeant Daniels escorted Kittinger up the four steps which led to the gondola and squeezed him inside. Then, while he held his breath, they clamped his nose, and lowered the helmet over his head. As soon as they had attached it firmly to the horse collar, Kittinger's new air supply began to flow. Then the men withdrew, and the anti-glare curtain was erected around the upper part of the gondola. The envelope above *Excelsior* tugged restlessly upwards towards the brightening sky. The dawn silhouettes of the Sacramento mountains were staggeringly beautiful. Kittinger prepared himself to leave them.

———

Inside the weather van, Duke Gildenberg was not a happy man. The reason for his concern was a storm front brewing in the neighbouring state of Texas. He was unable to rule out the possibility of it drifting towards southern New Mexico. He felt reasonably sure that, if this were to happen, the clouds would do nothing worse than interfere with the optical tracking of Kittinger's progress, but once again, he was in an invidious position. If he cancelled, he would be the villain. If he didn't, he might wind up with blood on his hands.

Gildenberg's powers of predicting weather patterns were the stuff of legend. On one occasion, he had promised a team conducting a dummy parachute test at Holloman that, if they assembled in his office after the launch, he would lead them to within a hundred yards of the mannequin's landing point. They had been somewhat taken aback to find themselves sitting around in an extended silence while Gildenberg twiddled his thumbs. Then, after several minutes, he had glanced at his watch, nonchalantly ambled over to a window and opened the blind. Immediately, the parachute had appeared, landing not a hundred yards from them. They had all been suitably impressed.

With a record like that, Gildenberg had no choice but to

respect his own instincts. This time, at the last moment, he decided to abort the flight. He was almost relieved when he learned that the message had arrived at the launch site moments too late. The matter was now beyond his control.

———

Almost as soon as the gondola lifted from the desert floor, Kittinger became aware of a problem. Once again, as he was heading for the stratosphere, he was having radio trouble. This time his UHF radio was not working properly. This did not in itself comprise an insuperable problem – Kittinger was still able to communicate with the ground through the back-up HF system – but it was inconvenient. His vocal communications would now have to share a waveband with the data that was constantly telemetered back to earth about his breathing and pulse rate. For the remainder of the flight, his heartbeat and respiration would be continually relayed back to him through his headphones, establishing a potentially alarming biofeedback loop. More importantly, the radio failure meant that a crack had appeared in the system right at the outset. This was scarcely a good omen.

As Marvin Feldstein, the project medical officer, wrote later in his report, Kittinger was not a man who found it easy to submit his destiny to machinery. His career was premised on his ability to take the steps necessary for his own survival. If a thoroughly tested piece of equipment could fail so early in the trip, who was to say that other, more vital items might not also pack up? When Ground Control established contact with Kittinger at 5000 feet, they found him noticeably testy.

In the normal course of events, Kittinger would have avoided looking up at the sky at this stage in his journey, just as a rock-climber would tend to avoid looking down.

To do otherwise was to risk inducing an inverted form of vertigo. But on this occasion, the temptation was irresistible. He didn't like what he saw. Later, he described it thus: 'Several miles high, an intruder had pushed its way into the mission. Spoiled was the promise of those flawless heavens. A layer of stratus, gossamer-thin and permitting visibility through its tenuous mass, stretched at 15,000 feet across the entire sky.'

Kittinger passed through those intrusive clouds right at the point at which he became reliant on his artificial air supply.

From the earliest times, people had been dimly aware that respiration became more difficult with altitude. In the fourth century BC, Aristotle noticed a tendency towards breathlessness among pilgrims climbing Mount Olympus. Four hundred years later, a Chinese general who had led a military expedition through the Karakoram range wrote the first recognised description of mountain sickness: 'South of Mount Pishan, the travellers have to climb over Mount Greater Headache, Mount Lesser Headache, and the Fever Hill, where they will develop a fever, turn pallid, feel a headache and vomit. Similar symptoms also occur in asses and other animals without exception.' Yet despite such observations, there was, in Europe at least, a striking failure to extrapolate the general rule that air becomes thinner with altitude. It can't have helped that there was no mountain higher than 16,000 feet in the entire continent, nor that there was little occasion to try to go up it.

This unfamiliarity with the loftier regions of the Earth was eventually corrected as one of the consequences of colonialism. In 1590, a Spanish Jesuit priest named José de Acosta suffered agonies while crossing a high mountain pass in the

Andes, and held nothing back in describing them:

When I came to the top of this mountain, I was suddenly surprised with so mortal and strange a pang that I was ready to fall from the top to the ground. I was surprised by such pangs of straining and casting as I thought to cast up my heart too; for having cast up meat, phlegm and choler, both yellow and green, in the end I cast up blood with the straining of my stomach. To conclude, if this had continued, I should undoubtedly have died. I therefore persuade myself that the element of air is there so subtle and delicate as to be not proportionable with the breathing of man, which requires a more gross and temperate air.

What Acosta was experiencing was altitude sickness or hypoxia, an oxygen deficiency in the body caused by the lungs becoming incapable of delivering enough of the gas to the blood. At altitudes higher than 10,000 feet, people unaccustomed to the reduced atmospheric pressure may become short of breath or experience dizziness. For those accustomed to living at or close to sea-level, the first symptoms of this condition can kick in even earlier. By 15,000 feet, the unacclimatised are likely to feel seriously unwell, with symptoms including vomiting, irrational behaviour and acute headaches caused by fluid leaking into brain tissue from the blood. At 18,000 feet, atmospheric pressure will have fallen to about half what it was at sea-level. At 25,000 feet, it will be down to just a quarter.

The earliest aeronauts were therefore right to be wary of ascending too far although, as has already been mentioned, there was confusion as to whether it was absolute distance from sea-level that mattered, or merely distance from the ground. As the fuss over the damaged cockerel had shown back in 1783, there was a major preoccupation with suffocation. Such fears were quickly allayed, however, when people started coming back from mountain-like altitudes with nothing worse than the odd frozen extremity. This might have generated a false sense of security.

One of the first men to push matters to the limit was Gaspard-Étienne Robertson (1763–1837), a colourful Belgian showman, who was, variously, a politician, physician, journalist, poet, singer, aeronaut and illusionist. Always one to dream big, Robertson first came to public attention in 1796, when he submitted to the French Directoire a scheme for destroying the British Royal Navy. The idea was to use giant mirrors to incinerate the enemy fleet by focusing the Sun's rays on it. His next venture was to set himself up as the proprietor of the 'Room of the Phantasmagoria', a horror show set in the crypt of an abandoned Capuchin nunnery outside Paris. Inside, with the aid of a primitive, candle-lit projector, Robertson would terrify his audiences with a series of ghostly images cast on to a gauze screen. At the end of the show, he would promise to reveal what he described as 'the only real horror', which awaited them all. Then an image of a beautiful young woman on a pedestal would appear, only to be suddenly transformed into a skeleton by some slick work behind the projector. The Capuchin order, with its morbid preoccupation with death, would certainly have approved.

Robertson was quick to latch on to any new trend, but it was ballooning that really caught his fancy. In 1803, he wrote on the subject with an optimism that was, at first sight, entirely reasonable: 'We have everything to hope and to expect from time, from chance, and from the genius of man. The difference which there is between the canoe of the savage and the man-of-war of 124 guns is perhaps as great as that between balloons as they are now and as they will be in the course of a century.'

To do his bit to hasten this predicted evolution, he then designed one of the most preposterous aerial vessels in history, before submitting the plans to 'all the Academies of

Europe'. The *Minerva* was to be a veritable city in the sky, 150 feet across and weighing in the order of seventy tons. Facilities would include an observatory, a theatre, a kitchen, a gymnasium, several 'closets' and even a church. An enormous barrel of German beer would be suspended beneath her, both for refreshment and to be used as expendable ballast in the event of an emergency. The plan was to transport sixty individuals on a research flight lasting half a year, in the course of which they would visit every corner of the globe and of the element above it. To avoid the need for her ever to descend, the *Minerva* would be equipped with several smaller, spare balloons for side trips to Earth. And if she should run into trouble and fall into the sea, the problem would not be insurmountable: the gondola could also function as a ship.

Despite these extravagant dreams, the balloon with which Robertson actually equipped himself was *L'Entrepenant*, purchased from the French Army when Napoleon disbanded the world's first airborne division in 1799. At this stage, some people still believed that ballooning might reveal laws exact enough to render meteorological phenomena as predictable as eclipses. Robertson, of course, was one of them. On 18 July 1803, with a music teacher named Lhoest, he embarked from Hamburg on the first balloon trip expressly for the purpose of making scientific measurements at altitude. The following is an extract from his later account of the journey:

I rose in the balloon at nine a.m., accompanied by my fellow-student and countryman, M. Lhoest . . . At 10.15, the barometer was at nineteen inches, and the thermometer at three above zero. We now felt all the inconvenience of an extremely rarefied atmosphere coming upon us, and we commenced to arrange some experiments in atmospheric electricity. Our first attempts did not succeed. We threw over part of our ballast, and mounted up till the cold and the rarefaction of the air became very troublesome.

During our experiments we experienced an illness throughout our whole system. Buzzing in the ears commenced, and went on increasing. The pain we felt was like that which one feels when he plunges his head in water. Our chests seemed to be dilated, and failed in elasticity. My pulse was quickened, M. Lhoest's became slower; he had, like me, swelled lips and bleeding eyes; the veins seemed to come out more strongly on the hands. The blood ran to the head, and occasioned a feeling as if our hats were too tight. The thermometer continued to descend, and, as we ascended, our illness increased, and we could with difficulty keep awake. Fearing that my travelling companion might go to sleep, I attached a cord to my thigh and to his, and we held the extremities of the cord in our hands. Thus trammelled, we had to commence the experiments which I had proposed to make.

In the aftermath of the flight, Robertson claimed that *L'Entrepenant* had peaked at 23,526 feet. Unfortunately, his track record and his famously well-developed powers of imagination made it difficult for his contemporaries to believe him. The reliability of his claims was further compromised by the fact that, in the early days of ballooning, all estimates of altitude were made by comparing barometric pressure on the ground with that in the air. No allowance was made for meteorological variation: it was assumed that atmospheric pressure would be constant at any given altitude. This over-simplification inevitably had an adverse effect on accuracy. It was also hard to have much faith in measurements taken by individuals when frozen or hypoxic.

The Paris Academy of Science eventually concluded that Robertson and Lhoest had gone no higher than 21,400 feet. Many years later, the great balloonist Henry Coxwell would show that a balloon of *L'Entrepenant*'s dimensions could only have reached the claimed altitude if all of the ballast had been jettisoned *en route*. By this stage, so much gas would have spilled from the neck that a safe landing would have been impossible. It was not until after Robertson's era that balloonists realised that the trick when aiming for extreme heights was to only partially fill a very large envelope with the lifting agent, to allow for expansion as the surrounding pressure fell with altitude.

The following summer, a rather more reliable set of scientific flights was made in France by the young chemist Joseph Gay-Lussac (1778–1850) and his companion J. B. Biot (1774–1862), the well-known physicist. They measured the highest ascent, conducted by Gay-Lussac alone, at 23,000 feet above sea-level. In the light of their experiences, the two men made a prescient assessment of the true nature of the dangers awaiting the high-altitude balloonist in their subsequent report to the Galvanic Society:

We have known for a long time that no animal can with safety pass into an atmosphere much more dense or much more rare than that to which it has been accustomed. In the first case it suffers from the outer air, which presses upon it severely; in the second case there are liquids or fluids in the animal's body which, being less pressed against than they should be, become dilated, and press against their coverings or channels. In both cases the symptoms are nearly the same – pain, general illness, buzzing in the ears, and even haemorrhage. The experience of the diving-bell has long made us familiar with what aeronauts suffer. Our colleague [Étienne Robertson] and his companion have experienced these effects in great intensity. They had swelled lips, their eyes bled, their veins were dilated, and, what is very remarkable, they both preserved a brown or red tinge which astonished those that had seen them before they made the ascent. This distension of the blood vessels would necessarily produce an inconvenience and a difficulty in the muscular action.

Not that the message was received in all quarters. Some

argued that exposure to high altitudes was positively healthy. In 1850, the American John Wise, author of *The History and Practice of Aeronautics*, advocated 'sending chronically diseased persons through the healthy fields of life-inspiring air above the earth'. As a balloon rises through the atmosphere, he wrote:

... there are two causes acting in beautiful harmony upon the invalid, calculated to produce the most happy results. While the most sublime grandeur is gradually opening to the eye and the mind of the invalid, the atmospheric pressure is also gradually diminishing upon the muscular system, allowing it to expand, the lungs becoming more voluminous, taking in larger portions of air at each inhalation, and these portions containing larger quantities of caloric, or electricity, than those taken on the Earth, and the invalid feels at once the new life pervading his system, physically and mentally ... the brain receives and gives more exalted inspirations, the whole animal and mental system becomes intensely quickened, and more of the chronic morbid matter is exhaled and thrown off in an hour or two while two miles up of a fine summer's day, than the invalid can get rid of in a voyage from New York to Madeira by sea.

There was evidently a fine line between the therapeutic and the dangerous.

———

For the first fifty years or so of the nineteenth century, the balloon's potential usefulness as an instrument of scientific research was largely overlooked. After the promising start made by the likes of Robertson and Gay-Lussac, the sport started to drift into the hands of showmen, who knew exactly how to exploit its inherent theatrical qualities. This growing association between ballooning and show-business tended to alienate the high-minded Victorian scientist. But this was to change in 1862, when the British Association for the Advancement of Science decided to finance a detailed study of the upper atmosphere.

The two men chosen to participate were the forty-three-year-old Henry Coxwell, and James Glaisher FRS, ten years his senior. Coxwell (1819–1900) was a greatly respected aeronaut who had started life as a dentist before taking to ballooning under an alias for fear of parental disapproval. Glaisher (1809–1903) had never gone near a balloon prior to the summer of '62. But he was the head meteorologist at Greenwich, and was filled with determination to 'make the balloon a philosophical instrument, instead of an object of exhibition, or a vehicle for carrying into the higher regions excursionists desirous of excitement, mere seekers after adventure'.

As will shortly become apparent, Coxwell and Glaisher embodied the contemporary ideal of stoicism to an almost comical degree. But it was this quality that would enable them to penetrate the realm of the jumbo jet in little more than their Sunday best. They were men on a mission, and nothing would be allowed to deflect them from their path.

In order to minimise the chances of their balloon being blown out to sea, Coxwell and Glaisher selected Wolverhampton in the heart of the British Midlands as the venue for the planned series of launches. The city was easily accessible by rail and had a gasworks handy to provide the necessary lifting agent.

The agenda drawn up for the flights by the British Association was a daunting one. One of its main items was a systematic testing of the then prevailing theory that the temperature invariably dropped 1°F for every 300 feet risen. The aeronauts would, in addition, measure the concentrations of water vapour at various levels, conduct sundry electrical experiments, test for ozone, observe the behaviour of magnets at different altitudes, collect air samples and take measurements of the solar spectrum. The balloon constructed for the purpose had a capacity of 90,000 cubic feet and was made of American cloth. It would later be known as the *Mammoth*.

The first launch in the series took place on 17 July, in circumstances that Glaisher described, with some understatement, as 'by no means cheering to a novice who had never before put his foot in a balloon'. A terrible gale was blowing, which made it impossible to secure any of the scientific instruments in their places prior to lift-off. Then, for the first minute after Coxwell released the restraining rope, the *Mammoth* moved only horizontally. But eventually she started to move skywards, and before long enough evidence had been accumulated to explode the neat temperature/altitude theory for ever.

At 19,135 feet, Glaisher found himself suffering from palpitations, and his hands and lips were dark blue. Two thousand feet later, he described a feeling 'analogous to sea-sickness', even though the gondola was perfectly steady. He was therefore greatly relieved when Coxwell initiated descent, having noticed that the balloon had drifted uncomfortably close to the North Sea. Unfortunately, the fabric of the envelope accumulated so much condensation on the way down, while passing through a cloud layer a mile and a half thick, that *Mammoth* became seriously overweighted. She fell so rapidly that she 'assumed the shape of a parachute', and most of the scientific instruments were broken on landing.

The second flight, on 18 August, was a much more tranquil affair. At 12,000 feet, Glaisher rhapsodised about the cloudscape below him, with its 'mountain scenes of endless variety and grandeur'. He was then treated to the beautiful sight, familiar to experienced balloonists, of the shadow of his vehicle cast on to the cloudbank beneath, surrounded by a rainbow aura. More disquieting were claps of thunder heard at 20,000 feet, by which stage the sky beneath was cloudless.

This time the balloon reached an altitude of 24,000 feet, with Glaisher, already somewhat acclimatised, faring better than he had before.

These flights were impressive in themselves, but it was the third ascent, on 5 September, that would catapult Coxwell and Glaisher into ballooning immortality. For the occasion, Mr Thomas Proud, manager of the Wolverhampton gasworks, had brewed a particularly potent supply of coal gas, chosen over hydrogen for reasons of safety. This batch promised to provide much more lift than usual.

The weather that day was overcast, and it was only at 11,000 feet that the balloon emerged into the sunlight. 'On emerging from the cloud at seventeen minutes past one,' wrote Glaisher, 'we came into a flood of light, with a beautiful blue sky without a cloud above us, and a magnificent sea of cloud below, its surface being varied with endless hills, hillocks, mountain chains and many snow-white masses rising from it.' Onwards they surged into a Prussian blue sky. They knew they were getting high when the live pigeons they tossed from the basket from time to time began to drop like frozen chickens. Glaisher described what happened after the balloon passed 26,000 feet:

Up to this time I had experienced no particular inconvenience. When at the height of 26,000 feet I could not see the fine column of the mercury in the tube; then the fine divisions on the scale of the instrument became invisible. At that time I asked Mr Coxwell to help me to read the instruments, as I experienced a difficulty in seeing them. In consequence of the rotary motion of the balloon, which had continued without ceasing since the Earth was left, the valve line had become twisted, and he had to leave the car, and to mount into the ring above to adjust it. At that time I had no suspicion of other than temporary inconvenience in seeing.

In fact, the cause of Glaisher's blindness was the dearth of oxygen now reaching his optic nerves. Before long, the same problem affected his limbs:

Shortly afterwards I laid my arm upon the table, possessed of its full vigour; but directly after, being desirous of using it, I found it powerless. It must have lost its power momentarily. I then tried to move the other arm, but found it powerless also. I next tried to shake myself, and succeeded in shaking my body. I seemed to have no legs. I could only shake my body. I then looked at the barometer, and whilst I was doing so my head fell on my left shoulder. I struggled, and shook my body again, but could not move my arms. I got my head upright, but for an instant only, when it fell on my right shoulder; and then I fell backwards, my back resting against the side of the car, and my head on its edge. In that position my eyes were directed towards Mr Coxwell in the ring. When I shook my body I seemed to have full power over the muscles of the back, and considerable power over those of the neck, but none over my limbs. As in the case of the arms, all muscular power was lost in an instant from my back and neck.

Glaisher was now in the throes of extreme hypoxia, but such was his sang-froid that he still managed to keep track of his impressions:

I dimly saw Mr Coxwell in the ring, and endeavoured to speak, but could not do so; when in an instant intense black darkness came over me, and the optic nerve lost power suddenly. I was still conscious, with as active a brain as whilst writing this. I thought I had been seized with asphyxia, and that I should experience no more, as death would come unless we speedily descended. Other thoughts were actively entering my mind when I suddenly became unconscious, as though going to sleep. I could not tell anything about the sense of hearing: the perfect stillness of the regions six miles from the Earth – and at that time we were between six and seven miles high – is such that no sound reaches the ear.

Just before Glaisher fell unconscious, Coxwell removed his thick gloves to make it easier for himself to manipulate some sandbags into a pile. He needed this to stand on if he was ever going to get to the tangled valve line. Unfortunately, when he placed his hands on the iron ring between the gondola and the envelope with the intention of hauling himself up into the rigging, they were savagely bitten by frost. He explained later to his companion what had happened next:

Mr Coxwell told me that in coming from the ring he thought for a moment that I had laid back to rest myself; that he spoke to me without eliciting a reply; that he then noticed that my legs projected, and my arms hung down by my side. That my countenance was serene and placid, without earnestness or anxiety, he had noticed before going into the ring. It then struck him that I was insensible. He wished then to approach me, but could not, and he felt insensibility coming over himself. He became anxious to open the valve, but, in consequence of having lost the use of his hands, he could not; and ultimately he did so by seizing the cord with his teeth and dipping his head two or three times.

This drastic remedy did the trick. The *Mammoth* began to descend, and the aeronauts immediately started to feel better. 'No inconvenience followed our insensibility,' as Glaisher drily put it. The balloon eventually landed in uninhabited country, and its record-breaking occupants were forced to walk between seven and eight miles to find suitable accommodation in which to recover.

The next task was to determine just how high the *Mammoth* had climbed. At peak altitude, one of its occupants had been unconscious while the other was frantically trying to revive him. Therefore no one had been watching the barometer at the key moments. To try to get round this problem, Glaisher carefully reconstructed the order of events before subjecting them to his acute powers of deduction:

My last observation was made at 29,000 feet, about fifty-four minutes past one. I suppose two or three minutes elapsed between my eyes becoming insensible to seeing the fine divisions and fifty-four minutes past one, and that another two or three minutes elapsed before I became unconscious; therefore I think that took place about fifty-six or fifty-seven minutes past one. Whilst powerless I heard the words 'temperature' and 'observation', and I knew Mr Coxwell was in the car, speaking to me, and endeavouring to rouse me; and therefore consciousness and hearing had returned. I then heard him speak more emphatically, but I could not speak or move. Then I heard him say, 'Do try; now do!' Then I saw the instruments dimly, next Mr Coxwell, and very shortly I saw clearly. I rose in my seat and looked round, as though waking from sleep, and said to Mr Coxwell, 'I have been insensible.' He said, 'Yes; and I too, very nearly.' I then drew up my legs, which had been extended out before me, and took a pencil in my hand to note my observations. Mr Coxwell informed me that he had lost the use of his hands, which were black, and I poured brandy over them. I resumed my observations at seven minutes past two. I suppose three or four minutes were occupied from the time of my hearing the words 'temperature' and 'observation', until I began to observe. If so, then returning consciousness came at four minutes past two, and that gives about seven minutes of total insensibility.

On the basis of these calculations, Glaisher estimated that the *Mammoth* had reached the astonishing height of 37,000 feet. While there was some debate about the exact figure within scientific circles, there was general agreement that Coxwell and Glaisher had exceeded 30,000 feet, and no doubt at all that they had pushed right at the limits of human endurance.

The next stage was a systematic study of the effects of altitude on human physiology. The man who would carry it out was Paul Bert (1833–6), professor of physiology at the University of Paris. Bert first became interested in the way changes in atmospheric pressure affected the body after observing the strange symptoms suffered by Parisian caisson workers. These men were responsible for laying the deep-water foundations of bridges. To do this, they worked at the bottom of rivers in inverted chambers, or caissons, filled with pressurised air to keep out the water. When they returned to the surface, they often experienced excruciating pain in their joints. This gave them a painful gait reminiscent of the 'Grecian Bend', a fashionable, stooping style of walking affected by contemporary women. Accordingly, the condition became known as the bends.

Back in 1667, Sir Robert Boyle had come close to identifying the cause of this syndrome when he noticed a bubble forming in the eye of an unlucky viper when he rapidly removed the air from its tank. But it was Bert who established the exact mechanism behind the bends. If a person was subjected to a too-swift reduction in pressure, the nitrogen dissolved in their blood would expand to form bubbles, which would then wreak havoc on the system. Bert therefore recommended that caisson workers ascend slowly at the end of their shifts to give their bodies time to acclimatise. In doing so, he ensured his place as the father of diving medicine.

Bert's study of what happened to the body as it ascended through one medium, namely water, naturally inclined him to consider the effects of its moving up through another – the air. He knew from the experiences of Coxwell and Glaisher that oxygen starvation would eventually became a major problem, but he now wanted to establish the precise parameters. To do this, he began by observing the demise of small animals in evacuated bell jars, some originally filled with ordinary air, some with pure oxygen, and others with a mixture of the two. From these experiments Bert found that the critical factor was not so much the overall pressure inside the bell jar at the moment of death as how much of it was exerted by the oxygen component. If this figure fell below a certain level, the haemoglobin in the blood would not saturate properly. He concluded that death occurred whenever the partial pressure of oxygen fell below 1.38 inches of mercury, irrespective of the proportion of the gas in the atmosphere. (Later, this figure would be revised somewhat downwards.) Because oxygen comprises only about 20.9 per cent of the atmosphere, the implication was that a person breathing pure oxygen could expect to function effectively at just a fifth of the pressure he would require if he was inhaling everyday air.

In order to extend his study to human beings, Bert next constructed the world's first man-sized decompression chamber. At the time and in its own way, his creation was as remarkable as a time machine. Within its walls, a person could 'virtually' travel to the bottom of the ocean or the top of the sky. In February 1874, Bert spent over an hour inside his new creation at a simulated altitude of 16,000 feet, noting the effects of hypoxia on himself and experimenting with relieving the symptoms with oxygen. Later he passed many happy hours in the chamber searching for the ideal pressure at which to deliver laughing gas (nitrous oxide) to induce anaesthesia.

Two of the most willing guinea-pigs for Bert's subsequent tests were Theodore Sivel and Joseph Crocé-Spinelli. With the backing of the French Society for Aerial Navigation, they intended to mount an assault on Coxwell and Glaisher's altitude record, with Gaston Tissandier. Tissandier, the celebrated balloonist, had become a national hero during the siege of Paris in 1870 through flying news out of the city and thus bypassing the encircling Prussians. Sivel and Crocé-Spinelli were professional scientists. The differing levels of experience and acclimatisation would have a determining influence on the fates of the crew members.

During a simulated ascent to 20,000 feet, the aeronauts noted the 'disagreeable effects of decompression and the favourable influence of superoxygenated air'. At Paul Bert's suggestion, they therefore decided to equip their balloon, the *Zenith*, with oxygen-enriched air. This was suspended from the rigging in spherical pouches made from cows' intestines. The gas, which was kept at ambient pressure, was to be inhaled through a mouth tube via a humidifier. This contained an aromatic liquid to moisten it and take away its ghastly taste. When in use, the devices looked like technicolour speech bubbles.

The *Zenith* took off on her record-breaking attempt on 15 April 1875. At 23,000 feet, Tissandier wrote (barely legibly): 'My hands are frozen. I am all trembling with cold. We are all right. Fog on the horizon, with little rounded cirrus. We are ascending. Crocé pants; he inhales oxygen. Sivel closes his eyes. Crocé also closes his eyes. Sivel throws out ballast.'

This was not, under the circumstances, the brightest thing Sivel had done in his life. He cut three bags of sand, and the balloon rapidly gained altitude. Tissandier tried to grab one of the oxygen tubes, but was too weak to move his arm, although his mind was still as clear as Glaisher's in similar circumstances thirteen years before. He also found that his tongue was paralysed. Before he passed out, he noticed that Crocé-Spinelli's head was inclined to one side, and that 'he seemed oppressed'. Sivel, meanwhile, was gesturing enigmatically towards the sky.

Tissandier recalled later that 'About the height of 25,000 feet, the condition of stupefaction which ensues is extraordinary. The mind and the body weaken by degrees, and imperceptibly, without consciousness of it. No suffering is then experienced; on the contrary, an inner joy is felt like an irradiation from the surrounding flood of light. One becomes indifferent . . . one ascends and is happy to ascend. The vertigo of the upper regions is not an idle word . . .'

These symptoms are uncannily reminiscent of scuba divers' descriptions of the 'raptures of the deep'. Among novices, this condition typically kicks in about 130 feet (40 metres) beneath the surface. Afflicted individuals suddenly feel light-headed, as if they were warmly and pleasantly drunk. They then start to feel drawn downwards, as if in the grip of a deliciously seductive magnet. If they fail to resist this pull, they will die. Clinically, they are suffering from nitrogen narcosis. Often confused with the bends, this is caused by abnormal quantities of nitrogen dissolving in the system as a result of the great pressure of water at depth, then interfering with nerve synapses. This did not apply to the occupants of the *Zenith*, although oxygen deprivation was having a similar effect. But as anyone who has ever experienced the raptures will tell you, there is undeniably a psychological component to the phenomenon. It is connected to leaving the familiar world far behind and therefore feeling free of its constraints. This was just what the men in the *Zenith* were going through.

At 1.30 p.m., Tissandier noted the time, closed his eyes, and sank to the floor of the basket, 'inert', as he later put it. The next thing he knew it was almost ten past two, and the balloon was falling rapidly. Sivel and Crocé-Spinelli were slumped unconscious. Tissandier managed to cut one bag of ballast to try to arrest the rate of descent, then went into a seizure and passed out. He was awoken a second time to the sound of a tremendous wind, a sign that the *Zenith* was now plummeting terrifyingly fast. The now revived Crocé was indiscriminately hurling equipment from the basket – ballast, rugs, even the heavy aspirator, which he had unhooked. Once again Tissandier passed out, as the balloon continued its crazy yo-yoing. When he came round, his companions were dead. Their faces were black and their mouths were filled with blood.

The ground was now approaching at great speed. Tissandier realised with horror that he was unable to locate the knife he needed to release the balloon's anchor at the moment of impact. Now half demented, he threw out two last bags of ballast, dropped to all fours, and scrabbled around for the missing blade, howling his dead friends' names all the while. Moments before the balloon hit the ground, he found it. But though Tissandier managed to cut the anchor loose in time, his ordeal was not yet over. So violent was the landing that he let go of the valve line, and the still-inflated *Zenith* was dragged across the fields by the wind. Inside the gondola, Tissandier and his cadaverous colleagues were shaken around together like dice in a cup. Eventually, he managed to catch hold of the valve line and bring the nightmare to an end. Then he got out of the balloon, and collapsed in a dead faint.

At the joint funeral of Sivel and Croce-Spinelli, Paul Bert delivered a rousing eulogy: 'They leap up and death seizes them, without a struggle, without suffering, as a prey fallen to it on those icy regions where an eternal silence reigns. Yes, our unhappy friends have had this strange privilege, this fatal honour, of being the first to die in the heavens.' Yet the two men had died unnecessarily. If they had been equipped with face masks, they would have survived. In the event, they had perished within feet of the life-sustaining oxygen tubes, too weakened by hypoxia to reach for them and save their lives.

The lessons of the *Zenith* disaster were of particular interest to a Viennese physiologist named Hermann von Schrotter. On 4 December 1894, breathing compressed oxygen via a face mask designed by von Schrotter, Arthur Berson of the Prussian Meteorological Institute took a balloon successfully to 30,000 feet. On 31 July 1901, he took off again in the 300,000-cubic-foot *Preussen*, attempting with his colleague Reinard Süring to surpass Coxwell and Glaisher's forty-year-old altitude record. Despite von Schrotter's recommendation, they insisted on breathing via tubes with pipe-stem mouthpieces. The decision almost proved fatal. After reaching a world record altitude of 35,500 feet, they initiated descent just before Süring collapsed unconscious. Berson soon followed him. At this point, the reasoning behind von Schrotter's earlier mistrust of the manual breathing system became all too apparent. Now that they were unconscious, the aeronauts were quite incapable of keeping the mouthpieces of their breathing tubes clamped between their lips, thus rendering them useless. Fortunately, the balloon was already on a downward course. Both men regained consciousness at around 20,000 feet, revived by the natural increase in oxygen, and were able to execute a well-controlled landing. They later declared that they had reached 'the greatest height at which human existence is possible'.

After the ascent of the *Preussen*, Süring and von Schrotter sat down to calculate the limits of human tolerance to altitude, both with and without supplemental oxygen. They realised that in the event of a high enough ascent, even pure oxygen would give inadequate protection against hypoxia. Von Schrotter estimated that above 41,000 feet, pressurised breathing equipment would be needed to maintain adequate blood oxygenation. He also prophesied the eventual construction of pressurised 'hermetically sealed' gondolas to take men beyond this limit. But until someone worked out how to build such a gondola, there would be an absolute ceiling on the activities of aeronauts.

These were the numbers working against high-altitude balloonists at the start of the twentieth century: breathing pure oxygen at 34,000 feet is equivalent to breathing regular air at sea-level. Above 40,000 feet, 100 per cent oxygen must be under positive pressure to maintain conditions equivalent to those at 10,000 feet on the ground. If the partial pressure of oxygen falls below 2.4 pounds per square inch, the blood fails to saturate properly. And at 43,000 feet, 100 per cent oxygen would be delivered to the body at 2.4 p.s.i. Sixty years on, as *Excelsior III* surged towards this critical line in the sky, Joe Kittinger was about to enter territory where, without artificial pressure, even pure oxygen would not be enough to save him.

Chapter Nine

PRESSURE

As Kittinger approached the boundary at 43,000 feet, he knew that his continued survival now depended on the effective functioning of a tiny piece of equipment buried in the seat beneath him. If all went according to plan, a mechanical sensor would detect the drop in the surrounding pressure and spring into life. A small valve would open, releasing liquid oxygen into a tortuous length of tubing ultimately connected to the pilot. As the gas started to boil (at $-297°F/-183°C$), it would flow into Kittinger's partial-pressure suit, causing it to stiffen. The suit was not unlike an all-over version of the inflatable armbands used to take blood pressure. Once activated, it would squeeze his body tightly enough to duplicate conditions inside a pressurised capsule. If, that was, everything went according to plan . . .

Sure enough, just as the altimeter registered 43,000 feet, Kittinger felt the reassuring bear hug of the partial-pressure suit kick in. This, he knew, would keep his lungs absorbing enough oxygen to allow him to function efficiently. But it was not the only reason for him to be thankful for the successful inflation of his suit. As Kittinger was acutely aware, breathing difficulties are merely the tip of the iceberg of problems posed by falling pressure at altitude. Much more sinister is the tendency of bodily fluids to start to boil.

All mountaineers are familiar with the phenomenon of water boiling more readily the higher they climb. This is a consequence of a reduction in atmospheric pressure: there is simply less weight pressing down on the water molecules to hold them in place. What few consider is that the pattern does not simply cease at the level of the highest mountain. The boiling point of water continues to fall, eventually reaching the level of normal human body temperature. At this point, known as the Armstrong Line in honour of the aeromedic who first identified it, the bodily fluids of an unprotected aeronaut would start to vaporise. Above 63,000 feet, the demands on protective equipment are essentially the same as those required for survival in a genuine vacuum. As Kittinger moved through the ever-thinning atmosphere, it was difficult to ignore the imminence of the moment of truth.

Prior to the 1930s, the life-antagonistic region through which Kittinger was now passing was inaccessible. Until somebody found a way to fulfil von Schrotter's prediction by constructing a viable hermetically sealed gondola, the problems posed by declining air pressure above 43,000 feet would keep a lid on human vertical progress.

The first man to slam into this ceiling was a hearty American Army Air Service captain named Hawthorne Gray, back in 1927. During that year, Gray made a series of research ascents from Scott Field Air Base in Belleville, Illinois, intent on surpassing not only Berson and Süring's ballooning mark, but also the absolute altitude record of 40,809 feet, set in an aeroplane by the Frenchman Jean Callizo.

Gray's approach to the business of high-altitude ballooning now seems to have been naïve to the point of recklessness, but he was unquestionably brave. Certainly, he was willing to learn things the hard way. His first ascent, on 9 March, almost ended in disaster. At 27,000 feet, the oxygen system froze, swiftly rendering Gray unconscious; when he awoke, the balloon was falling dangerously fast. Then he found, to his horror, that his knife was too blunt to cut open the sandbags that contained his ballast. In sheer animal panic, Gray ripped them apart with his bare, frozen hands. This was enough to make sure that the landing was merely violent, but it was not an experience he wanted to repeat.

In the light of this drama, Gray made changes to his plans for the next attempt. This time, the oxygen system would be kept well heated, and the pilot would be able to drop ballast simply by tugging on a ripcord. The little ballast that remained, that was, for Gray was hell-bent on the record, and he wanted the balloon's weight kept to an absolute minimum.

On 4 May 1927, an exultant Gray climbed nearly 7000 feet beyond the point that Süring and Berson had declared the highest at which human existence was possible. At 42,240 feet, the sky was 'magnificent in the depth of colouring, which was a deep, almost cobalt blue'. But although he had left the Earth well protected against the terrifying cold of the stratosphere, wrapped in thick layers of deerskin and wool, he had no way of compensating for the falling outside pressure. Out of nowhere, a sharp pain seared through his chest. The frightened Gray immediately initiated descent, but soon found himself unable to control it. In his determination to get to an altitude of eight miles, he had sacrificed too much ballast. The falling balloon accelerated, and at 8000 feet, Gray resigned himself to the inevitable. He climbed on to the lip of the basket and parachuted down, even though he knew that the official altitude record would now be withheld.

Six months later to the day, Gray took off from Scott Field for a third and final time. To keep himself company during his lonely ascent, he tuned his radio to a local jazz station. By the time he reached 30,000 feet, the temperature was −40°F/−40°C, and the balloon's clock had ground to an icy halt. When Gray threw out an oxygen cylinder for ballast, it snapped off the now-brittle radio antenna, leaving him alone in a silent world. At 40,000 feet, Gray scribbled in his logbook, 'Sky deep blue, Sun very bright, sand all gone.' And that was his final communication with his home planet. The next morning, he was found dead in an oak tree in Sparta, Tennessee. The official line was that he had somehow severed his oxygen hose between 43,000 and 44,000 feet, the peak altitude registering on the recovered altimeter. The *New York Times*, however, speculated that death had occurred when Gray's internal organs ruptured, due to insufficient outside pressure.

If the pressure barrier was ever to be overcome, it was evidently going to take some inspired lateral thinking. The man to provide it was an oddball Swiss physics professor from the University of Brussels. Auguste Piccard (1884–1962) didn't merely conform to the stereotype of the absent-minded professor: in many ways, he created it. When the great Belgian cartoonist Hergé wanted a model for Professor Calculus, the unworldly genius who bumbles his way through the Tintin books, he had no need to look beyond Piccard for his inspiration. Tall, thin, bird-like, with a mop of unkempt hair, Piccard had no regard for his physical appearance. His mind was somewhere else.

Where Piccard's thoughts were in the early 1930s was up in the still-virgin stratosphere, flying around in the domain of the cosmic ray. If cosmic rays were little understood during David Simons' era in the 1950s, they were, of course, still less so in Piccard's day. Nevertheless, or perhaps as a result, they were something of a holy grail for the physicists of the period. There was a simple reason for this. In the absence of the yet-to-be-invented particle accelerator, cosmic rays were the only possible source of raw material for the study of high-energy particles. Or, to put it another way, they promised to unlock the secrets of the atom.

Piccard knew that cosmic rays were far more abundant in the upper atmosphere than down on the ground because most of them were inevitably intercepted by air molecules long before they got to the Earth's surface. The question was, how to access this particle bonanza. For Piccard, who with his twin brother Jean had served in the Swiss Army's Lighter-than-Air Division during the First World War, the answer was obvious. He would go there in a hydrogen balloon.

With a background such as his, Piccard was never likely to approach the task ahead in the hit-or-miss manner of Hawthorne Gray. 'The modern scientific seeker should not cast himself head foremost into these perils,' he announced. 'The sport of the scientist consists in utilising all that he knows, in foreseeing the dangers, in studying every detail with profound attention, in always using the admirable instrument of mathematical analysis wherever it can shed its magical light upon his work.'

What made Piccard such a compelling figure was that this careful and methodical approach was only a part of his personality. He was also a flamboyant self-publicist. The public and the media loved him. However, he was not to everyone's liking, particularly those stiffer elements who resented his theatricality and his refusal to play by the rules. One disgruntled rubber manufacturer was particularly candid: 'My own personal dislike for . . . Piccard started when it came to my attention that he wore inverted chicken baskets as helmets. The day he came to the Goodyear plant, he bounced around all over the lot and insisted on drinking from the laboratory spigots instead of the drinking fountains in the hall.'

There was little doubt that Piccard enjoyed his celebrity, and he played up to the crowd. But his passionate individuality not only captured the public imagination: it led him to a solution to the problem that had been arresting mankind's upward progress for more than a generation.

Piccard's genius was to see the analogy between the atmosphere and the oceans, and to exploit it imaginatively in a way that no one had before. He began with the observation that much the same thing was required of the hypothetical stratospheric vehicle as was called for in a submarine. In both cases, the environment inside must be protected from the life-threatening conditions outside. In the case of a submarine, this protection could only be achieved by building thick metal walls to prevent the machine being crushed by the weight of the surrounding water. A balloon capable of lifting such a payload would have to be implausibly large. But there should be no such weight problem with a capsule designed to head upwards because, in the ever-thinning air, the pressure inside would always be greater than out. All that was required was a craft robust enough to resist the temptation to explode under such circumstances. It should certainly be possible to build a sealed capsule light enough for a balloon to carry into the stratosphere. And, as an added bonus, the greater internal pressure would make sure the doors stayed shut.

With the backing of the scientifically curious king of the Belgians, Piccard set to work on the practicalities of his pet project. A spherical aluminium gondola seven feet in diameter with two hatches and several three-inch portholes was designed and commissioned, based on the kind of apparatus used in beer-brewing. Its shape was intended to minimise wind resistance and to provide the greatest strength and least weight for the quantity of space enclosed. To facilitate temperature control, one side was painted white and the other black. If the capsule were to become too cold during its forthcoming odyssey, it could be rotated by means of a special motor to present its dark, heat-absorbing face to the sun. If, on the other hand, it were to overheat in the fierce solar glare, its white, reflective face could be put forward. Or that at least was the idea.

With characteristic verve, Piccard addressed himself to the question of ballast. The limited space dictated that something far denser than the usual sand had to be chosen, but it was important that it should pose no threat to the people down below. Piccard's solution was to position himself under an industrial chimney while various grades of lead shot were poured over his head. He eventually pronounced himself satisfied and undamaged by what he described as 'lead sand'.

On 27 May 1931, the FNRS (*Fonds National de la Recherche Scientifique*) was launched from Augsburg in Germany, a location chosen for its considerable distance from the sea. Piccard and his assistant Paul Kipfer entered the gondola in the preposterous headgear that so annoyed the man from Goodyear. The first they knew that the ascent had commenced was when Kipfer spotted a factory chimney disappearing beneath them.

When the FNRS reached a height of two and a half miles, Piccard heard an ominous whistling coming from somewhere in the gondola. He and Kipfer frantically scanned the walls of the capsule with their ears to locate the leak. Fortunately, Piccard had catered for this eventuality. The tiny hole was duly found, and plugged with a mixture of petroleum jelly and oakum (the shredded fibre from old ropes). To bring the air pressure inside the cabin back up to its previous level, he simply dribbled some liquid oxygen onto the floor.

After twenty-eight minutes, the balloon had reached a world-record altitude of 51,000 feet. The FNRS had been tear-shaped at launch, but she was now a perfect sphere, glowing in the golden light of the sunrise. But almost immediately a second problem became apparent. The motor designed to rotate the gondola was not working properly, and the capsule, unable to move its reflective side towards the sun, was starting to overheat. As the temperature inside the capsule rose to 104°F/40°C, Piccard and Kipfer were reduced to eating the frost formed by pouring more of the precious liquid oxygen into an aluminium beaker to slake their thirst. The pale blue liquid was so cold (−297°F/−183°C) that water vapour in the cabin's atmosphere instantly condensed and froze on the sides of the beaker.

A still more serious consequence of the rising heat was that the rubber seals around the hatches began to warp. The whistling in the capsule was now terrifying. Air pressure could be maintained through a mixture of strategic patching up and topping up with liquid oxygen, but not indefinitely. The situation worsened considerably when it became apparent that the rope operating the release valve on the *FNRS*'s envelope was not working. The pair were now prisoners of the stratosphere.

Back on Earth, concern mounted for Piccard and Kipfer when they failed to return at noon as planned. The evening newspapers solemnly printed their obituaries. But ten miles above the Earth, the two men remained very much alive. Their ingenuity was certainly undiminished. At one stage, a barometer was broken, sending beads of mercury marbling across the floor. The scientists knew that by stripping away the thin layer of protective oxide, the liquid metal was capable of eating straight through the aluminium walls. If only they had a Hoover . . . Then Piccard had a brainwave. He attached a length of rubber tubing to a small tap mounted on the wall of the capsule, and turned it on. The tube, now directly linked to the stratosphere, was instantly transformed into an improvised vacuum cleaner. It ravenously sucked up the mercury. Kipfer watched through a porthole as the metal streamed out of the capsule.

The hope that sustained the two scientists through their long day in the stratosphere was that as the Sun went down, the gas in the *FNRS* envelope would contract, allowing the balloon to descend. To their great relief, this was exactly what happened. In the middle of the night, they touched down on the Obergurgl glacier in the Austrian Alps. As they descended the following day, they called out to a team of rescuers heading in the opposite direction. The rescuers ignored them. Their hearts were too heavy with the thought of the two dead bodies they expected to find in the capsule.

The *FNRS* capsule remained on the glacier for almost a year before it was recovered. In the meantime, work began on a replacement for Piccard's next assault on the stratosphere. This time, it was prudently painted entirely white. For this attempt, launched from Zurich, Piccard was accompanied by another assistant, Max Cosyns. Paul Kipfer's family had prevailed upon him, understandably, not to put them through a second such ordeal. Nevertheless Kipfer was an eager spectator to the ascent, or at least he thought he was. It later transpired, much to his embarrassment, that the shining object on which he had focused his telescope throughout the flight had not in fact been *FNRS* but the planet Venus.

In a somewhat different corner of the sky, Piccard and Cosyns sat shivering inside a gondola transformed by the extreme cold into a crystal grotto that bristled with tiny needles of ice. In the rarefied atmosphere of the stratosphere, the cosmic ray counters fired away almost continuously. The noise was like a shower falling on a tin roof. But the *FNRS* was beyond the reach of weather. Her peak altitude was a new world record of 53,152 feet.

Having stretched the boundaries of human exploration upwards with *FNRS*, Auguste Piccard now turned his attention to the conquest of the deep. His eventual solution, the bathyscaphe, would be another triumph of analogical thinking. The process of descending to the bottom of the sea then coming back up again, Piccard realised, was much the same as taking a round trip in a balloon. It was just the order of events that differed. In one instance, you started at the top, while in the other you began at the bottom. But in both cases the vehicle needed to be heavier than its surroundings on the way down and lighter on the way up. The machine Piccard came up with would therefore, in effect, be an underwater balloon, but one designed to pass through a medium several hundred times thicker than air. In place of hydrogen, its gasbag or 'float' was filled with lighter-than-water aviation fluid, and iron shot was used as its ballast.

Piccard's withdrawal from the ballooning scene left no shortage of candidates to surpass the mark he had drawn in the sky. In the aftermath of the ascents of *FNRS*, the United Press Agency announced that 'Six world powers have begun a race for supremacy in the stratosphere – that freezing region ten miles above the Earth where airplanes can attain the speed of bullets.' The USA and the Soviet Union in particular were spurred by Piccard's achievement into a frenzied game of ideological king-of-the-castle.

The two emerging superpowers had related but very different reasons for engaging in this battle for the atmospheric high ground. In the USSR, the exercise was all part of the propaganda offensive through which Joseph Stalin sought to convince the world (and terrorise his own people into believing) that the Soviet Union was a thriving, modern, industrialised nation. In depression-ravaged America, on the other hand, the imperative was to bolster faith in the power of the corporate state. There was an urgent need for inspiring public projects for the battered population to rally round.

Like the Babylonians before them, both the USA and the USSR would find answers to their dilemmas in the grand vertical statement. In America, this tended to take the form of the skyscraper – the Chrysler Building was completed in 1930 and the Empire State Building the following year. But both nations shared a loftier ambition. They began to contest the human altitude record in much the same way as they would later fight for the Moon. Ostensibly the goals were scientific but, not for the last time, what was really at stake was the supremacy of a way of life.

The first throw of the dice was made by the Americans in a highly publicised attempt timed to coincide with the 1933 World's Fair in Chicago. The organisers had originally invited Piccard himself to pilot the hubristically named *Century of Progress*, while the 'Conqueror of the Stratosphere' was touring the country earlier in the year. But Piccard had declined, instead recommending his twin brother Jean, who didn't have a balloonist's licence and would therefore need to be accompanied by a qualified pilot. If anything, Jean was even more eccentric than Auguste, although he was equally brilliant. With his tousled hair and distinctive gait, he was the kind of man people turned to look at in the street. The first-choice candidate point-blank refused to work with him. His place was therefore taken by Tex Settle, a naval lieutenant commander with the broken-nosed profile of a boxer, and the only man ever simultaneously qualified to fly aeroplanes, gliders, blimps, rigid airships and free-balloons. Settle also found Jean Piccard a handful, and in due course he managed to persuade the organisers that it might be better if he made the trip alone.

On 5 August, amid much razzmatazz, the *Century of Progress* was launched from Soldier's Field in Chicago in front of 20,000 expectant spectators. At the cry of 'Up ship!', the gondola began to rise with Settle still hanging jauntily out of the porthole. Searchlights followed the great balloon until it looked like a tiny ascending light-bulb, but the crowd had no way of knowing that all was not well up there.

Shortly after take-off, as was standard procedure, Settle had valved some gas to control his rate of climb. Unfortunately, the valve had promptly jammed in the open position. The balloon scarcely got to 5000 feet before Settle was forced to make an embarrassing emergency landing, coming down in a railway yard less than two miles away. The envelope was torn to pieces by rampaging souvenir-hunters.

As a result of the *Century of Progress* fiasco, the USSR was quickest off the starting-blocks in this dress rehearsal for the Space Race, just as it would be when it came to the real thing. In the early autumn of 1933, Georgi Prokofiev, Konstantin Godunov and Ernest Birnbaum reached an altitude of 62,300 feet in the *Stratostat*. The event provided a welcome escape for the pent-up emotions of a population downtrodden by the demands of Stalin's latest five-year plan, and the scenes of jubilation in Moscow were comparable to those in America after Lindbergh flew across the Atlantic in 1927. Four months later they would be replaced by scenes of mass mourning.

On 20 November, Tex Settle finally made it to the stratosphere, in the company of Major Chester Fordney of the US Marines. On this occasion, the launch was kept low-key to avoid the possibility of another humiliation. The *Century of Progress* lifted up from Akron, Ohio, a stone's throw from the giant hangars that housed the Goodyear-Zeppelin Company's airships. The ground crew, aware that the aeronauts intended to conduct experiments to investigate the effects of cosmic radiation on the reproductive systems of fruit-flies, had thoughtfully left them a packet of sanitary towels in case they should find themselves changing sex. This time, the *Century of Progress* made it unscathed into what Settle evocatively described as 'the region of night beyond the Earth's atmosphere'. The balloon came tantalisingly close to the Soviet record, but missed out by 1067 feet.

Back in the USSR Stalin, irritated by the near-success of the Settle/Fordney flight, ordered a new Soviet effort to coincide with the 17th All-Party Congress at the end of January 1934. The balloon in question was a monster, five times larger than the *Century of Progress*, built and manned by three civilian engineers: Pavel Fedosienko, Andrei

Vasenko and Ilya Uhsyskin. She was called *Osoaviakhim 1* – literally 'Society for the Promotion of Aviation and Chemical Defence', perhaps the least romantic name in the history of ballooning.

By the middle of the morning of 30 January, the proto-cosmonauts were high in the stratosphere, reporting an unprecedented altitude of 67,585 feet. At 4.07 p.m., there was a final, garbled communication from *Osoaviakhim*: 'The bright sunlight . . . the gondola . . . beautiful sky . . . the ground . . . this . . . the sky . . . the balloon . . . it . . .' Then the balloon began to fall. In their determination to establish a new record, the crew had deposited far too much ballast. They had nothing left to jettison to slow down the descent. *Osoaviakhim* fell so fast that the ropes connecting the gondola to the envelope started to snap. Finally, the two components separated at 1500 feet. The capsule hit the ground like a meteorite, and its occupants were killed instantly.

Barographs showed that Fedosienko, Vasenko and Uhsyskin had reached a peak altitude of 72,178 feet, nearly two miles higher than any previous ascent. Their ashes were solemnly interred in the walls of the Kremlin, as Stalin and his prime minister, Molotov, looked on. The mourning was the most intense since the death of Lenin. In the days that followed, hundreds of thousands of Muscovites filed past to pay their respects. Many no doubt felt a twinge of guilt, for these men had died pursuing the dreams of a nation.

The people of America only narrowly avoided a similar experience when the next stratospheric mission was launched from their soil. *Explorer I* was the brainchild of Captain Albert Stevens, the dashing Army photographer who had parachuted from the then inconceivable altitude of 26,500 feet back in 1924 (see Chapter Seven). *Explorer*, built by the Goodyear-Zeppelin Company and financed by the National Geographic Society, was half the size of the *Hindenburg*, with an envelope three times as capacious as that of any previous free-balloon in America. Stevens was to be accompanied by two experienced Army balloonists: Major William Kepner, equipped with a fashionable toothbrush moustache, and the gangly Captain Orville Anderson, who looked like an elongated version of Gandhi.

After scouring the western United States for a suitable launch site, Kepner and Anderson finally settled on a curious gouge in the Earth's crust, hidden within the Black Hills of South Dakota. This feature, carved out by swirling waters millions of years before, came to be known as the Stratobowl. It consisted of a broadly circular five-acre patch of grass surrounded by cliffs 400–500 feet high. Because of this topography, the Stratobowl could provide a unique degree of shelter for the delicate task of inflation. It was a balloonist's fantasy and, as a result, it became the Cape Canaveral of its era.

Explorer I began propitiously enough, with a troop of curious local Native Americans arriving in full regalia to give the project their blessing. The launch, on the morning of 28 July 1934, also went smoothly. But as the balloon approached the Soviet altitude record of 62,300 feet, a problem emerged that dramatically illustrated the perils of the stratosphere. As millions of rapt Americans listened to a live radio broadcast of the ascent, Major Kepner reported some dispiriting news: a large tear had appeared in the fabric of the envelope. 'The bottom of this balloon is pretty well torn out and it is just a big hole in the bottom here. I don't know how long she is going to hold together.'

Naturally, it wasn't long before *Explorer* started to plummet. Inside the pressurised capsule, the flight's three participants had no alternative but to sit back and endure the ride until the balloon reached an altitude where they could begin to contemplate opening the hatches without consigning themselves to the certainty of a grisly death. As Stevens later recalled: 'No one made a move toward the lever. To have opened it would have meant almost instant unconsciousness from change of pressure. Our tissues would have expanded suddenly, somewhat as would those of certain fish drawn hurriedly to the surface from ocean depths, and the results would have been both distressing and disastrous.'

Explorer continued to hurtle earthwards. At 5000 feet, just as the passengers were preparing to bail out, a friction spark from the tearing fabric of the balloon ignited the remaining hydrogen in its envelope, and what was left of *Explorer* exploded. The capsule was now in free-fall. In a finale that would have stretched credibility in a cartoon, all three aeronauts managed somehow to parachute to safety: Anderson from the relative luxury of 3000, Stevens from 2000 and Kepner from a mere 500 feet above a rapidly expanding Nebraska cornfield. It could have been much worse: as he had tried to leave the gondola, for one agonising moment the large-framed Stevens had found himself stuck in the hatch.

In the light of this catalogue of near-misses, various changes were incorporated into the design for *Explorer II*. To pre-empt the problem of spontaneous combustion, it was decided to use a new lifting gas, the inert helium, for the first time. Because helium was not as light as hydrogen, the balloon's envelope would need to be even more prodigiously enormous than its predecessor, at 3.7 million cubic feet. Even then, to ensure a record altitude, it would be necessary to reduce the payload by leaving Major Kepner behind. The hatches were widened, too, in consideration of Stevens' posterior.

By dawn on 11 November 1935, *Explorer II* was ready for action. In temperatures approaching 0°F/−18°C, onlookers watched as a small bump began to appear in the centre of the laid-out envelope, a vast circular expanse of fabric stretched out on a bed of sawdust and fringed with spotlights. Bit by bit, to the sound of almost seventeen hundred hissing cylinders of compressed helium, they saw it morph first into the shape of a giant pie, then of a medusa jellyfish, and finally of a vast inverted sack held down with guy-ropes. Then, at 8 a.m., the monster lifted off.

Despite the technological sophistication of the mission, Anderson and Stevens had a refreshingly amateur feel about them, with their borrowed football helmets and packed sandwiches. This did not, however, prevent them establishing a record, at 72,395 feet, which would stand for over twenty years. At peak altitude, Albert Stevens took the first photographs to prove beyond any doubt that the Earth was indeed curved. When *Explorer II* landed, near White Lake, South Dakota, her envelope was cut up into hundreds of commemorative bookmarks. The United States would go into the Second World War as undisputed king-of-the-castle.

In the summer of 1960, Kittinger was the first balloonist since Hawthorne Gray to pass through the pressure barrier without the protection of a pressurised capsule. He knew well that nothing stood between him and the deepening surrounding vacuum but his thin, standard-issue partial-pressure suit. He was already paying the closest attention to his helmet pressure gauge, with the memory still uncomfortably vivid of what had happened to him during the first Excelsior flight. Now he had passed 43,000 feet, Kittinger added monitoring the performance of his pressure suit to his regular checklist.

As he approached 50,000 feet, he stretched his limbs almost as a reflex, feeling for the reassuring resistance of the suit. To his acute dismay, he realised that his right glove had failed to inflate properly. Somehow, the tube that connected the glove to the rest of the pressure-suit system must have cracked after leaving the jealous care of Sergeant Daniels.

Kittinger knew what this meant. As he ascended into the ever-increasing vacuum above, blood would start to pool in the vulnerable area, interfering with its circulation. Tiny pockets of air trapped beneath his skin would start to inflate, causing it to balloon. His hand would swell grotesquely and then it would grow agonisingly cold. He dreaded to think what would happen at 63,000 feet, the point at which the boiling point of water would fall to normal human body temperature. He was reasonably certain that the pressure exerted by his skin and the walls of his blood vessels would prevent his hand actually exploding, but the experience was not going to be comfortable.

(During the mid-1960s, a test subject at NASA's Manned Spacecraft Center was accidentally exposed to a near vacuum when his space suit sprang a leak in a decompression chamber. He remained conscious for about fourteen seconds, roughly the time it took for the now oxygen-deprived blood to travel from his lungs to his brain. He regained consciousness when the pressure inside the chamber was restored to the equivalent of 15,000 feet. He reported that just prior to passing out, he had felt the saliva on his tongue begin to boil.)

His first dilemma was whether or not to inform Ground Control. If he did so, it was a foregone conclusion that Dr Feldstein would order him to abort the flight. And if that happened, it was more than doubtful that permission would be granted for another Excelsior flight. The authorities had been reluctant enough to sanction this one. Under this scenario, scores of good men would have spent many months labouring in vain. The Beaupre parachute might never be live-tested, and untold numbers of future stratonauts might die unnecessarily as a result. Looking at it this way, there was scarcely any choice to make. Kittinger elected to stay quiet.

Later on, Joe Kittinger would maintain adamantly that this decision to proceed had had nothing to do with fearlessness.

On the contrary, he would confess that by this stage he had been thoroughly afraid. But his reactions had been, as he would later put it, predetermined. Only the imminent danger of death could have persuaded him to leave the gondola. That was what being a test pilot was all about.

Chapter Ten

THROUGH THE SKY

As *Excelsior III* approached 50,000 feet, the thermometer reading fell to an unearthly −94°F/−70°C, then levelled off. Joe Kittinger took little comfort from this halt in the previously relentless decline in temperature. The balloon itself, so flexible and ethereal at ground level, was now as brittle as a giant Christmas bauble. In this condition, any sudden strain might cause it to tear. And the stabilising temperature was unambiguous evidence that it was now entering the phase of the ascent where such strains were most likely.

The lowest level of the earth's atmosphere is known as the troposphere, from the Greek for 'region of mixing'. Within this region, air absorbs solar energy according to its water content, which declines with altitude. The warm, moist air at the lower levels of the atmosphere expands and rises, forming clouds when it has cooled sufficiently for condensation to occur. Meanwhile, its place at the surface of the Earth is taken by cooler, denser air, which in its turn is warmed and rises, and so on. The resulting pattern of circulation is known as convection. It is this engine that drives all the phenomena we know as weather.

Weather, however, as anyone who has flown in a commercial jet will have noticed, does not simply go on up for ever. In 1902, the French meteorologist Léon de Bort worked out why. After launching 238 sounding balloons, each carrying a thermometer to a preordained height in the sky (the point at which a balloon of that particular thickness would burst), de Bort concluded that the temperature of the atmosphere ceases to fall about eight miles above the ground. He named the zone above this height the 'stratosphere', a concept later refined to take into account the discovery that its boundary varied between ten miles at the equator and five at the poles. Within the stratosphere, temperature actually *rises* with altitude, owing to the increasing absorption of solar energy by ozone, that rare and much discussed gas. This reversed temperature profile brings an end to the process of convection and, with it, the ability of clouds to form.

Unfortunately for the unwary aeronaut, the troposphere, like the sea, is at its most potentially turbulent at its upper boundary. This is the so-called tropopause, where, in their dying flourish, the winds of the jet stream can gust at more than 200 m.p.h. It was at this point that Kittinger had been scared witless during Man High I. Fortunately, the jet stream was known to subside during the summer. There remained another problem, however. Other things being equal, a gas balloon will rise faster if the surrounding air is cold than if it is hot. Warmer air, in other words, has less 'lift'. Now, at the tropopause, a balloon quickly passes from a region in which the temperature is falling to one in which it is rising. The warmer air of the stratosphere therefore acts like a break. If a balloon is ascending too rapidly, it may billow alarmingly at this stage, as if it has struck a ceiling. In a sense, it has. Accordingly, around half of all high-altitude balloon failures occur here.

Kittinger had seen for himself what could happen to a balloon at the tropopause. On one occasion, staring through high-powered binoculars, he had seen a gasbag cut clean in two. Still more ominously, he had once seen a balloon rupture at a similar altitude then snarl itself around the emergency parachute, which attempted, forlornly, to return its payload safely to Earth.

It was with some relief, therefore, that after a few tense

minutes Kittinger noticed the temperature beginning to climb
– a sure sign that he had safely negotiated the tropopause.
As if to confirm the passing of a great barrier, a strange
kind of tranquillity descended on the scene. Indeed, things
were starting to feel distinctly other-worldly. In the dwindling atmosphere, a dreamlike silence pervaded. Around the
balloon, the familiar blueness was dissolving like a mirage.
Above, the sky grew darker and darker, in seemingly impossible defiance of the blazing sun. At 6.15 a.m., some forty-
five minutes into the flight, Kittinger was passing into the
stratosphere.

———

Until the 1930s, the entirety of human history was lived out
with the certainty that, if it was daytime and conditions were
cloudless, a blue sky would be arching overhead. Whatever
else could be said about this azure backdrop, it certainly
seemed to be permanent. It was not surprising, therefore, that
our ancestors took the 'common sense' view that the sky was
a solid dome, although 'common sense' scarcely does justice
to the awe in which they held it.

It must be remembered that before the discovery of mag-
nification people retained an implicit trust in the evidence of
their eyes. The sky was therefore taken to be just what it
appeared to be: a gigantic dome that touched the Earth at the
horizon. Indeed, many cultures explicitly believed that it was
possible to travel to the point at which the two realms met.
An official inscription documenting the Asiatic campaigns of
the Egyptian Pharaoh Thutmose III announces, 'His southern
frontier is to the horns of the Earth, to the southern limit
of this land; his northern to the marshes of Asia, to the
supporting pillars of heaven.' In the modern era, a resident
of the Mortlock islands, near Papua New Guinea, carefully
explained to a European anthropologist that it was impossible

to sail further west than the nearby Paloas islands because the sky then started to get too close to the ground.

Belief in the solidity of the sky appears to have been universal in the ancient world. It is still a feature of the mythology of several peoples, including the Lapps, who say that the Pole Star is a nail that holds up the entire sky and will continue to do so until the heavenly archer, Arcturus, shoots it down to bring about the end of the world.

Part of the explanation for the prevalence of the belief that the sky was some kind of lid lies in human psychology. Shelter is a fundamental need: if we are deprived of it for long enough we start to feel horribly exposed. This aversion unconsciously predisposed our forebears to interpret what they saw above as evidence that the sky was a canopy or a solid dome (the tent motif was particularly popular among nomads). The alternative view, that it just continued indefinitely, would have threatened to tip the believer into a cosmic agoraphobia of the most debilitating kind. In any case, that wasn't the way it *looked*. And before Copernicus, that argument usually won the day. (Revealingly, even in a world where we *know* the sky isn't solid, we continue to act as though it is for a variety of practical purposes. When it comes to locating targets with their telescopes, for example, astronomers rely on co-ordinates assigned to the heavenly bodies as if they were points on the inside of a gigantic sphere. The illusion runs deep.)

Those who wanted more tangible evidence for the solidity of the sky could find it in the few treasured items that had, over the ages, indubitably fallen from the heavens. Many cultures took the understandable view that such objects were stray pieces of a rocky or metallic sky, sent as gifts from the gods. But the most accessible reason for believing in the hardness of the heavens was the unchanging appearance of the constellations. As utterly unfathomable as the stars might be, there was no denying that something was holding them in place, at least relative to each other. The obvious explanation was that they were set in a vast, rotating dome.

To the Babylonians, the sky was the upper half of the body of the primordial sea monster Tiamat, slain by the god Marduk at the creation then cloven in two. The lower half of the body was then used to form the world. The Ancient Egyptians believed that the sky was made of iron. They called this material *be-ni-pet*, or 'sky metal', and knew thunder as *khru-bai*, or 'sound of the metal', a phrase that expresses concisely how they understood it to be generated.

Other cultures were equally imaginative in their interpretations of what went on in the heavens. In an elaborate attempt to explain the colours of sunset and dawn, the Akkadians of Mesopotamia devised a heaven divided into three regions, each made of a different precious stone. The upper heaven was said to be made of 'Luludanitu, stone of Anu', which scholars have identified as a red mineral covered with black and white patches. The middle heaven, on the other hand, was made of blue 'Saggilmut' stone, with the god Bel enthroned in its centre on a dais of lapis lazuli. Below him lay a lower heaven of translucent jasper, on which he was said to have inscribed the stars.

For those in the Judaeo-Christian tradition, authority for belief in a solid sky was to be found in the first chapter of the book of Genesis. Here, on the second day of his creation, God is described as making a 'firmament' to divide two primordial oceans: 'And God made the firmament and separated the waters which were under the firmament from the waters which were above the firmament. And it was so. And God called the firmament Heaven.' (Genesis 1:7–8) Significantly, *raqia*, the Hebrew word translated as 'firmament', has the more usual meaning of a thin, beaten-metal plate. The identity of the waters under this cosmic divide becomes clear in the course of what happens next: Yahweh commands them to gather together to reveal the dry land, then gives them the name 'seas'. It is the other set of waters that is puzzling, at least at first glance. Clearly, we are dealing with a cosmology now thoroughly alien to us. It is only when we stop to reflect on the nature of the society that produced the Old Testament that clues start to emerge.

The Israelites were a pre-scientific people who lived in a desert environment by the sea. The water cycle, and hence the 'true' origin of rain, must have been a mystery to them. Clearly clouds had something to do with it, but it seemed most natural to assume that they were filled from above. Was not the sky blue, like the sea? And had there not once been a dreadful flood? Surely the vault of the sky held back another ocean, and Yahweh could open or close the hatches at his whim.

Several other passages in the Old Testament enshrine a belief in a solid sky. Take Exodus 24:9–10: 'Then Moses and Aaron, Nadab and Abihu, and the seventy elders of Israel went up, and they saw the God of Israel. Under his feet was something like a pavement made of sapphire, clear as the sky itself.' Or Ezekiel 1:22: 'Over the heads of the living creatures there was the likeness of a firmament, shining like awesome crystal, spread out above their heads.' The imagery may vary – clearly there was as yet no rigid doctrine on the matter – but the assumption is remarkably consistent, as it was throughout the ancient world.

Only in China does the theory appear to have been put forward that the sky was merely empty space. In about AD 180, the author Tshai Yung recorded the existence of three schools of astronomy. The *kai thien* school believed in a domed universe, and located the sky at a distance of about 80,000 li (or 26,666 miles) from the Earth. The *hun thien* movement adhered to a system of celestial spheres approximating to that of the Ancient Greeks. But there was also the school of *hsuan yeh* or 'infinite emptiness', who believed that the cosmos consisted of exactly that. In about AD 300, the historian Ko Hung wrote that all the original books of the *hsuan yeh* school had now been lost, but that one of the old imperial librarians recalled that they had believed that 'The Sun, the Moon and the company of the stars float freely in empty space, moving or standing still, and all of them are nothing but condensed vapour.'

This conception fitted in well with Buddhist and Taoist notions of impermanence and fluidity and, from a western perspective, it was remarkably ahead of its time. In 1595, the Jesuit missionary Matteo Ricci could still write home to Europe complaining of the 'absurdities' of the Chinese, such as their believing that there was one sky rather than ten, that it was empty and not solid, and that the stars were not, as any fool knew, attached to a firmament, but instead moved in a void.

Although the *hsuan yeh* astronomers had essentially got it right, the movement was an aberration in the grand scheme of history. However the conclusion was reached, the usual assumption was that a person travelling far enough would eventually bump up against a solid sky. To try to put this theory to the test would have been considered madness, even blasphemy. Nevertheless, there were tales in circulation of travellers reaching the point where the Earth and the heavens were joined, like the Buriat hero said to have shot an arrow through a gap that appeared between the two at sunset.

The idea that the sky was a solid vault might have seemed correct intuitively, but it couldn't account for the motions of all the heavenly bodies. The Sun, Moon and planets in particular followed paths strikingly different from those of the stars. It was this observation that led the Ancient Greeks to formulate an ingenious cosmology that would dominate thinking about the sky right up to the eighteenth century.

Since prehistoric times, people in the northern hemisphere had been aware that the so-called fixed stars revolved around Polaris, the Pole Star. The first refinement the Greeks had made to this notion was to specify that the stars were attached to something spherical. They had reached this conclusion by combining careful observation with two already deep-seated beliefs. The first, most clearly exemplified in the teachings of Pythagoras (582–507 BC), was that the universe was profoundly mathematical. The second, most famously espoused by Plato (c. 428–347 BC), was that the heavens were necessarily perfect and unchanging because they had been made by a perfect deity. And, of course, mathematically, the most perfect shape was the sphere. If a sphere was rotated once about any given axis, all the points on its surface would move in perfect circles, and end up exactly back where they started. Just like most of the sky.

The problem was that the planets often seemed to do anything but move around in nice regular circles. Even the Sun and Moon varied in where and when they emerged from the horizon. The first man to propose a scheme to reconcile these observations with the demands of religion and reason was Euxodus of Cnidus (c. 406–355 BC). His genius was to realise that the actual movements of the planets could be accounted for, at least to a then tolerable degree of accuracy, by assuming that they were moved by the combined actions of more than one sphere. All that was necessary was for the spheres to have differing axes of rotation. They could even revolve at unchanging speeds.

Euxodus' system required a total of twenty-seven interlocking spheres: four for each of the known planets (Mercury, Venus, Mars, Jupiter and Saturn), three each for the Sun and the Moon, and one for the stars. By the time the great Aristotle

(384–322 BC) had got his hands on the theory and elaborated upon it, the figure had risen to fifty-five. There was also another important clarification. Euxodus might merely have seen the spheres as a useful fiction – the evidence that survives leaves the question open – but with Aristotle, there were no such ambiguities. He explicitly believed that his spheres were physically real.

For Aristotle, as for most of his contemporaries, the universe was divided into two very different regions. The earthly or sublunary zone was characterised by change and decay, while the heavens were perfect and immutable. In support of this absolute division between the realms, he cited as evidence the way in which objects moved within them. In the heavens, as anyone could see, their motion was circular, whereas beneath the Moon, they usually moved in straight lines. (Whirlpools, apparently exceptions to this rule, are said to have troubled Aristotle so much that he once threw himself into one to find out more.) In a piece of inspired sophistry, the philosopher deemed circular motion to be perfect and eternal because, unlike linear movement, it had no contrary. In other words, a body moving in an anti-clockwise rather than a clockwise circle would still visit all the same stations. However, if it were to move left rather than right, or down instead of up, it emphatically would not.

To complement his understanding of how the Earth and the heavens behaved, Aristotle posited that there was a fundamental difference in the stuff they were composed of. In the sublunary sphere, he held that everything was made of the four elements in varying proportions: earth, water, air and fire. In a perfect world, which this demonstrably was not, these elements would arrange themselves in precisely that order, with earth at the centre and fire on the perimeter. As it was, things merely tended to fall into that sequence, according to which of their constituent elements predominated. Flames typically flickered skywards, gases bubbled up through liquids and solid items sank to the bottom. It was because of this spontaneous propensity of earthly substances to seek their natural levels within the vertical hierarchy that terrestrial objects tended to move in straight lines. (In the *Meteorologica* (*c*. 340 BC), Aristotle used clouds as a practical illustration of the workings of his system. They could not form in the 'upper air', he argued, because it was too near the realm of fire. Nevertheless, they were created by the 'intermingling' of elements that went with the imperfection of the sublunary sphere: the heat of the sun warmed water, converting it into something like air, which then rose to form clouds.)

The heavens were a very different matter. They were constructed of aether or 'quintessence', a transparent crystalline substance not to be found on Earth. This quintessence was itself organised into a series of concentric shells or spheres, whose purity gradually decreased with the approach of the corrupting influence of the Earth. Each had its own pattern of movement, and each was home to a particular heavenly body or variety thereof. The large number of interlocking spheres that Aristotle was forced to come up with in order to account for all the observable differences in the paths of celestial objects might have aroused suspicions had not the model turned out to work rather well. Certainly, no one before the Enlightenment was going to take much issue with what the philosopher placed on the outside of the final sphere: the shadowy, eternal figure of the Prime Mover himself.

In an Aristotelian world, then, our theoretical balloonist would begin his journey in air made cool and moist by its proximity to the realm of water. The higher he ascended, the hotter and drier it would become. As he approached the realm of fire, conditions would grow unbearable, until eventually he was incinerated. Even if he were somehow to survive, it would not be long before he came slamming up against an unseen, impenetrable barrier. Beyond this point, as an imperfect being, his very existence would be impossible. Indeed, during the Middle Ages, it was a favourite philosophers' game to speculate on the fate of a limb thrust through the outermost sphere.

Albert of Saxony, arguing in the spirit of Aristotle, claimed that nothing could be extended beyond the outermost sphere, because there would be no place or space there to receive it. Jean Buridan, a professor at the University of Paris in the early fourteenth century, begged to differ:

It would not be valid to say that he could not place or raise his arm there simply because no space exists into which he could extend his hand. For I say that place is nothing but a dimension of body and your place the dimension of your body. And before you raise your arm outside this last sphere nothing would be there; but after your arm has been raised, a place would be there, namely the dimension of your arm.

Although, as these speculations imply, Aristotle's cosmology came to be extraordinarily dominant – not least because the works of all the other major Greek philosophers were lost to the world during the Dark Ages – it was not without its weaknesses. In particular, it failed to give satisfactory explanations for two aspects of the behaviour of the 'wandering stars'. They could vary dramatically in brightness, and the outer planets – Mars, Jupiter and Saturn – sometimes abandoned their usual paths and started to move back on themselves in a process known as retrograde motion.

Despite these problems, the classical world's commitment to the idea that heavenly bodies must move in perfect circles was so deep that its philosophers were prepared to get themselves into terrible contortions to maintain this feature in their cosmological systems. Claudius Ptolemy of Alexandria (c. AD

100–170) produced the most important and accurate celestial almanac in antiquity, but the innovations he introduced to account for what he observed stretched the Aristotelian system to the limit.

The thin end of the wedge was the Epicycle, the supposed rotation of a planet about a fixed point on a larger circle which is itself rotating. For practical purposes, this concept worked very well, even providing a workable explanation of retrograde motion. A similar thing could be said of Ptolemy's next idea, the Eccentric, in which the Earth was considered displaced from the centre of a planet's still perfectly circular orbit. This hypothesis accounted brilliantly for observed variations in planetary speed and brightness, but it felt like an uncomfortable straying from the doctrine of geocentricity. But this was nothing compared to the consternation Ptolemy caused the purists when he introduced a final modification to preserve his system at the points where it was proving most tricky. This was the Equant, a purely imaginary point from which a planet would still look as though it was moving in uniform circular motion even if it wouldn't from Earth. It would take fourteen centuries to do it, but it was eventually the Equant that broke the camel's back.

In the words of the Pole Nicolaus Copernicus (1473–1543), it was the desire to find a way to dispense with the troublesome Equant point that first 'gave us the occasion to continue the mobility of the Earth'. As far as he was concerned, what the Ptolemaic astronomers had done was 'just like someone taking from various places hands, feet, a head and other pieces' and making from them 'a monster rather than a man'. It had all just got too complicated. And so, one day, Copernicus spawned a revolution simply by wondering whether it wouldn't be easier to suppose that the Earth went round the Sun.

In 1543, Copernicus' *De Revolutionibus Orbium Celestium*

('On the Revolutions of the Heavenly Spheres') was published. According to legend, the author's copy arrived while he lay on his deathbed. In his hands he now had an alternative answer to the vexing problems of retrograde motion and the varying brightness of the planets. If the Earth was also orbiting the Sun, it was only natural that it would sometimes be closer to a given planet than at others. Such a mechanism would also explain why the planets sometimes appeared to change direction: at certain points during the Earth's journey around the Sun, it would appear to overtake the outer planets travelling on longer and slower orbits. From the Earth's perspective, in other words, the planet would seem to go backwards.

It took some time for the consequences of Copernicus' book to filter through. At first, with the aid of a nervy publisher's preface, which claimed that what followed was never intended to be taken *literally*, his theory was welcomed as a nice intellectual exercise that also happened to yield useful results. The effectiveness of his system was also compromised by its dogged adherence to the doctrine that heavenly bodies must necessarily move in circles (it would be left to Johannes Kepler, 1571–1630, to show that they actually moved in ellipses). It was only when Galileo Galilei started to insist vociferously, in 1616, that Copernicus' model was literally true that the Vatican put its foot down. But by that stage, the old Greek cosmology had already received some mortal blows.

It had been essential to Aristotle's system that all unusual and transient phenomena in the sky be regarded as occurring on the Earthly side of the innermost sphere, that of the Moon. The premise that the heavens were unchanging demanded it. In 1572, however, the Danish astronomer Tycho Brahe (1546–1601) noticed what seemed to be a new star in the heavens. We now know that he was looking at a supernova.

Brahe analysed it using the embryonic technique of parallax, where changes in the apparent position of an object in the sky as the observer travels from A to B, or as the Earth moves round the Sun, are carefully measured in order to calculate its distance. This proved that the newcomer was well to the other side of the Moon.

Five years later, Brahe reached a similar conclusion about a comet, which had fortuitously chosen that moment to appear. There was now no doubt about it. The heavens could change after all. And as he tracked the path of this interplanetary visitor, he reached the inescapable conclusion that it was passing directly through the regions where the celestial spheres were supposed to be located. If they really had been made of a solid, transparent substance, the comet would surely have shattered them. The idea slowly began to take hold that the Earth and the planets were travelling freely in space.

Bit by bit, Aristotle's cosmology was being dismantled. In 1610, Galileo (1564–1642) became the first man to point a recently invented gadget called the telescope towards the sky. When he turned it on the Moon, he saw mountains and valleys and dark areas, which he took to be seas. This was a devastating discovery for man's ego. The world was not as unique as he had supposed. And then Galileo looked at Jupiter, and found that it, too, had a moon – four of them, in fact. So Copernicus had been right: celestial objects did not necessarily orbit the Earth after all.

All this was very bad news for the Greek understanding of the heavens, but it was not until 1684 that it finally gave way. In that year, Isaac Newton published *De Motu Corporum in Gyrum* ('On the Motion of Bodies in Orbit'), the result of years of meditation on the precise trajectories of the planets. In it, he proposed a revolutionary new force to account for the movements of heavenly bodies.

This was gravity, a mutual, mass-based attraction, which Newton argued held between all objects in the universe. Suddenly, there was no need to postulate the existence of vast, invisible structures to explain how the heavenly bodies were kept in their places. Newton had shown that they could manage this all by themselves. Aristotle's universe shook until it crumbled, and with it his notion of a solid, crystal sky.

————

So where did this leave the beautiful blue thing up above? As is so often the case, it transpired that the way forward had already been pointed out by Leonardo da Vinci (1452–1519). Even though he had died ahead of the Copernican revolution, Leonardo's fascination with light, fuelled by his endless curiosity and his search for verisimilitude in his paintings, had led him to the germ of an answer.

When Leonardo was asked how to add depth to a picture, his terse answer was to 'add a little blue'. Because he was such an acute observer, he knew that distant objects often appeared to be of that hue. Through a variety of experiments, including looking at sunlight as it passed through woodsmoke and steam, he reached a hypothesis to explain this phenomenon and wrote it down in his notebook: 'I say that the blueness we see in the atmosphere is not intrinsic colour, but is caused by warm vapour evaporated into minute and insensible atoms on which solar rays fall, rendering them luminous against the infinite darkness of the fiery sphere which lies beyond.' In another place, he explained that faraway mountains tended to look blue on account of 'the great quantity of air that lies between them and your eye'. It was almost as if there was a thin slice of sky between the observed and the observer. Clearly the process that coloured the heavens also applied horizontally.

Some of the earliest attempts to provide a properly scientific explanation of the blue colouration of the sky revolved around Isaac Newton's discovery, made while he was confined to his home during a local outbreak of plague, that white light could be split into the colours of a rainbow by a prism. Perhaps something in the upper atmosphere had a similar effect, and selectively sent the blue part of the spectrum of light in our direction, either by refraction (the bending of light when it passes from one medium into another) or reflection. In 1847, the German physicist Rudolf Clausius (1822–88) suggested that this something might consist of bubbles or 'vesicles' of water, although it was not clear how they were supposed to have made it to such heights. There was also the problem that the blue to be obtained by passing light through a prism was rather different from the one that prevailed in the sky.

A much more satisfactory explanation was provided by the Irishman John Tyndall (1820–93) towards the end of the 1860s. While experimenting with the ways in which light passed through a variety of gases and vapours, Tyndall found that when the particles of which they were composed fell within a certain size range, a cerulean glow would appear inside the glass tank that housed them. And to bolster the feeling that he had created an ersatz sky in his laboratory, when he peered back through the apparatus at the light source it looked red or yellow, like the Sun. Evidently what was happening was that when a beam of white light struck a sufficiently small particle, the blue component was scattered out of it while the rest of it kept going.

It is possible to duplicate the effect Tyndall had identified with a clear plastic bottle filled with a litre of water and one and a half teaspoons of milk. If a torch is shone through the liquid, the beam should look yellow when viewed from the other side of the bottle while overall the milk-water mixture should have a bluish tint. If the torch beam looks reddish, you've added too much milk.

This experiment works because of the presence of tiny particles within the milk called colloids. The same principle is at work when tobacco smoke appears blue in slanting sunlight. Tyndall realised that something similar must be going on in the sky. Particles in the atmosphere must be colliding with rays of light from the sun and scattering blue light everywhere. Inevitably, a portion of it would be directed downwards to human eyes from every corner of the heavens. So whichever way a person looked, the sky would still seem blue.

As well as explaining its daytime colour, Tyndall's experiments also showed why the sky appears red or orange when we look towards a sunset. When the Sun is close to the horizon, its rays have to pass through much more atmosphere to get to us than they do when it is directly overhead. This is because of their changed angle of approach. As a result, by the time sunlight reaches our eyes in the evening, most of the blue part of its spectrum has already been scattered away. And white light with the blue removed looks red.

John Tyndall would go on to analyse light scattering over central London in a pioneering investigation of atmospheric pollution. The man who would nail down a precise formula for the scattering he had observed was John William Strutt (1842–1919), later the 3rd Baron Rayleigh.

Born to a prominent family of Essex farmers, the young Strutt did not immediately show much promise. When he was first shown to his grandfather, the old man announced, 'That child will either be very clever or be an idiot.' Family legend is divided as to whether this remark was prompted by the shape of the child's head or the fact that he was three years old before he began to speak. Fortunately, the more optimistic prognosis would prove correct. Almost as soon as the child did start to talk, it was to ask questions such as what became of spilled water when it dried.

In 1871, Rayleigh reviewed Tyndall's findings in the light of the emerging theory that light behaved as a wave. He discovered that when a beam of light strikes a small enough particle, it is scattered to an extent inversely proportional to the fourth power of its wavelength. Or, to put it in slightly more everyday English, the shorter the wavelength (that is, the closer to the blue end of the spectrum) the greater the scattering. In other words, blue light gets scattered much more than red. About nine times more, in fact.

Early on in his career, Rayleigh avoided specifying what kind of particles he thought were responsible for the scattering in the sky. Tyndall had proposed that the culprits were tiny droplets of water or numerous specks of dust. However, there were problems with this suggestion. In the first place, such particles tended to be too large. Dust was more likely to scatter red light – a phenomenon observed after volcanic eruptions and in the atmosphere of Mars – while water droplets were typically big enough to scatter all wavelengths of light equally, hence the whiteness of clouds. Second, as scientists began increasingly to point out, if dust or water were really responsible for the appearance of the sky, its colour would vary much more with humidity and pollution than it actually did.

The idea gained currency that molecules of nitrogen and oxygen in the atmosphere were themselves large enough to generate the familiar blue sky. In 1899, Lord Rayleigh published a paper in which he endorsed this view. The previous year, while staring at Mount Everest from the veranda of a hotel in India, he had had a similar experience to Leonardo four centuries before him. Although the weather was particularly fine at the time, he noticed that the upper portions of the mountain were indistinct and bluish. He reasoned that a proportion of the light coming from them must have been scattered away by the time it got to him. On analysis, he found that most of the 'missing' light was blue. His findings led him to calculate, via methods too arcane for most laymen to follow, that the number of molecules in a cubic centimetre of air was around 3×10^{-19}.

It was not long before Rayleigh scattering was universally accepted by physicists as the correct explanation for the colour of the sky. The hypothesis of Sir James Dewar (1842–1923), the first man to liquidise oxygen, that the sky was blue because this was the colour of the gas in its liquid form, turned out to be a brief, if intriguing, red herring. It would remain for Albert Einstein (1879–1955) to calculate the detailed formula for the scattering of light by molecules, which is now considered to be the final word on the subject.

The work of men like Rayleigh and Einstein also offered an explanation for why the blueness of the sky can vary quite dramatically from place to place, even when conditions are equally cloudless. A major determinant is the amount of water vapour in the atmosphere. Water droplets are much larger than air molecules, so when a beam of light strikes one, all its wavelengths are likely to be scattered equally. When this happens, a whitish colour is generated. Airborne pollutants tend to have a similar effect. The consequence is that the sky appears more vividly blue the less moisture – or the fewer pollutants – it contains. This is usually the case in desert areas, but the principle also applies to mountains, as the water content of air tends to decline with altitude. At high elevations, there are also fewer air molecules overhead, and therefore less Rayleigh scattering. As a result, the blue of the sky is darker than it is at sea-level.

The cause of the daytime colour of the sky from an Earthly perspective was now resolved, but for anyone contemplating leaving the planet, there was one more important consequence of the theory of Rayleigh scattering. If you take away the atmosphere, or for that matter the light source, the sky will not be blue any more. Instead it will be inky black.

Although some of its deepest secrets were being unravelled, some misconceptions about the sky persisted for a remarkably long time. A case in point was an enduring paranoia about meteors. Well into the Victorian era, these were thought to burn up at far lower altitudes than is usually the case. As a result, balloonists who rose too high were thought to be in real danger of bombardment by enormous flying boulders. It didn't help matters when so eminent an aeronaut as Henry Coxwell, whose dental heroics featured in an earlier chapter, came across a meteor during one ascent. Years later, writing in 1887, he estimated that it had passed within six hundred feet, although, as he went on to admit: 'It is just possible that the apparent closeness of this meteor was illusory, and that the real distance was very many miles; its size was half that of the Moon, and I could not but feel that if such another visitor were to cross my path, the end of the *Sylph* and its master would be at hand.'

By 1960, however, a great many of the remaining gaps in our knowledge about the sky had been closed. It was known, for instance, that the Earth's atmosphere included, in addition to oxygen, nitrogen, water vapour, carbon dioxide and argon (a gas discovered by Rayleigh), minute quantities of neon, helium, methane, krypton, hydrogen, nitrous oxide, ozone and xenon. It was also known that the atmosphere was divided into several highly distinct vertical layers. The advent of high-altitude, instrument-bearing sounding balloons early in the twentieth century had revealed all kinds of data about conditions several miles above the ground. But some things were only ever going to be resolvable in person.

Not least of them was what would happen to somebody's mind up there.

As Kittinger entered the stratosphere, early in the seventh decade of the twentieth century, he did not come crashing into any crystal barriers; nor was he pelted by meteors. Some things, however, he found the ancients had got right. In particular, they had anticipated that this would be a realm of great serenity, where experience would be somehow purer and more 'real' than on Earth. In the language of their times, they had attributed this to greater proximity to the divine, rather than to a reduction in the distorting effects of the atmosphere, or to stability brought about by the temperature starting to increase with altitude. But the fact remained that they had guessed correctly.

Serene though the surroundings were, theirs was a disturbing tranquillity. For although the stratosphere undoubtedly held its attractions, they vied for supremacy in Kittinger's consciousness with an insistent and visceral fear. For the scientist-philosophers had also been right on another, highly pertinent point. This was emphatically not an environment designed with people in mind. Later he likened the experience to swimming in cyanide.

At 55,000 feet, Kittinger radioed down a description of his surroundings as 'hostile'. All around him, the fundamental concepts of terrestrial experience were starting to break down. A case in point was the temperature. Was it cold up here in the stratosphere or was it hot? The thermometer in the gondola read −36°F/−38°C; pretty chilly by anyone's standards. Yet parts of Kittinger were sweating profusely, while others were steaming like dry ice. It all depended on what was directly exposed to the beams of the Sun. One half of him could be literally baking while the other was deep-freezing in its shadow. The question just didn't make much sense any more. Kittinger simply gave thanks that the gondola was slowly rotating.

Another conceptual casualty of the extreme altitude was colour, although this was more a source of wonder than of fear. Freed from the scattering and muddying effects of the atmosphere, the light had a searing purity up here. It seemed to reveal the inner truth of everything it struck. For Kittinger, it was as though up until this moment he had been looking at life through a dirty lens.

Of all the phenomena reported by visitors to the strato-sphere, perhaps none is so tantalising for the earthbound as this transformative effect on colour. From the few pre-vious stratospheric ascents, Air Force medics had learned to expect otherwise taciturn military men to start gushing when confronted by this hyper-real colouring. David Simons had responded to it in mystical language. For Kittinger, in his open gondola, the experience was likely to be even more powerful. There were some among the ground crew who feared that it might prove too much for him. Alone in the vastness of space and far beyond reach of any possible assistance were anything to go wrong, it would be all too easy for a man in his position to freak out. Or to react to the sheer otherness of the environment by turning in on himself and freaking in.

Alone at the top of the sky, Joe Kittinger was about to come face to face with himself.

Chapter Eleven

DARK NIGHT OF THE SOUL

As the balloon approached 60,000 feet, she was travelling uncomfortably close to her drag limit. This is the point at which the rate of ascent, in combination with air resistance, threatens to tear open a balloon's envelope. In *Excelsior*'s case, the drag limit was 1400 feet per minute. Duke Gildenberg, watching the dials like a hawk back at Ground Control, radioed instructions for Kittinger to valve some gas. He immediately complied, slowing the climb rate from 1300 to 950 feet per minute.

Ever since he had left the troposphere, Kittinger had been too busy addressing the competing demands of his instrument panel and his stiffening right hand to pay much attention to his surroundings. Monitoring the pressure gauges of his suit and helmet had developed into a virtual obsession. It was impossible to dispel the illusion that it was only by concentrating on the needles of the dials that he kept them pointing to their life-maintaining positions. Now, as *Excelsior III* passed 80,000 feet, he forced himself to tear his eyes away from them. But he did not turn them, as might be expected, to the panorama he had so longed to drink in during Man High. Instead, he concentrated on the one view that really mattered to a parachutist: straight down. It gave him the shock of his life.

Twelve miles ago, the balloon had passed through a thin layer of cloud, which Kittinger had confidently expected the rising desert Sun to burn off. Now, as he looked down, he saw that it had congealed into a solid mass several thousand feet thick. At the sight of this tangible symbol of his separation, he felt himself flooded with rage. All manner of emotions had been building up inside him for the past half-hour. Previously, they had been kept in the background by his preoccupation with practical tasks. But now, ignited by the sight of the undercast, they flared up and threatened to overwhelm him.

It was not so much that he could no longer see the ground beneath him that so troubled Kittinger but the realisation that his colleagues could not see him. The knowledge that they could still track his movements with radar was of little consolation. What he needed right now was to be *visible*. Every cell in his body clamoured for this fundamental validation: 'It became intensely important to me that the Excelsior team on the ground visually follow my progress through the sky. But the clouds denied this to me. They had cut me off from the Earth, imprisoned me in a world where I was the only inhabitant, and blinded my friends on the ground.' Unless he could be seen by his fellow men, at least theoretically, it seemed as if he'd lost a cornerstone of his existence.

The perils of isolation had long been known through the experiences of shipwrecked sailors. Herman Melville in *Moby Dick* crystallised the phenomenon in the tale of a cabin boy named Pip, who falls overboard during a whale hunt and soon finds himself floating on the sea with nothing visible between himself and the horizon. When he is eventually picked up, several hours later, he has been transformed into a raving madman. Kittinger was not going mad, but he was, as he later put it, 'face to face with a stark and maddening loneliness'. In clinical terms, he was experiencing an acute form of separation anxiety. At no point since his birth could he have felt himself to be in such an alien environment or so exposed. As a consequence, the feelings that coursed through him had the primary power of the animal.

As shocked as he was by the violence of his reactions,

Kittinger was aware of a part of himself that stood outside their reach, observing them dispassionately. 'Through all this there came the startling realisation that I could, as if I were an observer studying my own mind, witness the onslaught and the effects of this shattering emotional need. It was so unusual as to startle me from the weight of the oppressing thoughts.' Someone who had come back from the brink of death might recognise this as the part of the personality that asserts itself in out-of-body experiences. A Buddhist or Hindu might equate it with the Atman, the 'True Self', which another individual might spend many lifetimes attempting to awaken. Under this interpretation, the extremity of Kittinger's circumstances had catapulted him directly to a point that he might only otherwise have reached through years of meditation.

Joe Kittinger, however, was not of a meditative cast of mind, nor was he going to arrive at the space equivalent of Nirvana without a struggle. As he came later to understand it, he attempted to make his inner turmoil tolerable by converting it into intellectual terms. He turned on himself, subjecting himself to a fierce self interrogation. Why had he let himself get into this situation? Why could he not identify the cause of his reactions, and thereby neutralise them? Kittinger fought the fire with the piece of equipment he knew best: his reason. But this time the fire was too big.

Back at Ground Control, Marvin Feldstein and Billy Mills detected that a change had come over their pilot at about 85,000 feet. They greeted it with some concern. It manifested itself in a series of long, descriptive monologues that seemed alien to the normally terse Kittinger. In them, he minutely detailed his surroundings and the strange colours of the stratosphere. To Marvin Feldstein, chief medical officer for the flight, this change in the wisecracking pilot he knew was a highly unwelcome development. At first, he feared that Kittinger had fallen victim to Breakaway Syndrome, the dangerous but seductive feeling of disconnection that Simons had wrestled with during Man High II. Then the penny dropped: Kittinger was talking incessantly to drown thoughts that would otherwise be unbearable. Their man in the sky was a long way from happy.

Sixteen miles overhead, Kittinger was starting to realise what might have seemed obvious to someone less well drilled in the application of reason to emergency. It was the sheer helplessness of his situation that was disturbing him so. He was a fish out of water, and it frightened him. Although he was only a few thousand feet higher than he had been in the previous Excelsior missions, this was an altogether different experience for him psychologically. Before, he had almost been able to convince himself that, in the event of his pressure suit failing, he had a fighter's chance of survival. If he had been forced to bail out at 75,000 feet, he might conceivably have fallen to a survivable altitude before the depressurisation had time to kill him. But now, for the first time in his life, Kittinger sensed that if anything were to go wrong with his equipment, he would be powerless to save himself. 'For the first time – the altimeter dial read more than 80,000 feet – I came to believe that I might not return safely to the Earth.'

This realisation profoundly challenged Joe Kittinger's sense of self. Being a test pilot was all about omnipotence, about convincing oneself that one could control anything. Now that illusion had been cruelly stripped away. In the emptiness of the stratosphere, Kittinger was confronted by the truth of the human condition in a super-concentrated form. We are alone. We are vulnerable. We are very, very small. Our lives are contingent on many fragile things, and death may strike at any moment. As he floated above the planet, Kittinger entered the dark, stratospheric night of his soul. He would never forget the agonies of self-recrimination he endured during those minutes. How could he have been so stupid as to believe he could cope with anything? He winced at the pain in his right hand and peered into the abyss of self-pity. 'My hand was cold, and all the pain I had not felt before coiled in it like a snake and struck.' And then, from crushing defeat, the seeds of a solution appeared.

It is never easy to fight the unknown. Which way should you turn? Hitherto, Joe Kittinger had experienced his surroundings as an increasing absence, in line with his intellectual knowledge of the stratosphere. Now, when he needed it, he remembered a tip his mentor John Paul Stapp had given him. Think of the vacuum as an active presence. Endow it with substance. Give it shape, and then you will be ready to deal with it.

This simple psychological trick changed everything for Kittinger. At last he could see what he was up against. The 'space' in which he was immersed was not mere emptiness, as the word might suggest to the earthbound. From the perspective of a man swimming in it, the void was a voraciously active killer. If there was the slightest chink in his armour, the vacuum of the stratosphere would ruthlessly exploit it. It was the antithesis of 'stuff' itself, and stuff was what Kittinger was made of. It was a fact, then, that he might easily die up here. His life depended on circumstances beyond his control, on his team back on Earth and on his equipment. He had no choice but to accept this. To emphasise the point to himself, he felt through his pressure suit for the entry nodes for the oxygen that kept it inflated. If the flow should stop, it would kill him as surely as if the blood were to freeze in his veins. The only way forward was to have faith. It always had been, and it always would be. It was just more obvious out here on the edge of space.

Confronted by this inescapable reality, Kittinger surrendered his life to the care of his colleagues and his equipment.

'Willingly, understanding the fear now, I entrusted my life to the hands of my team.' Everything that could have been done for him had been done. Suddenly he was suffused with peace. In the naked glare of the Sun, he had achieved a kind of enlightenment. Afterwards he wrote: 'I went back to work. I knew no burden now. You might say that I had found an understanding that few men are privileged to receive . . .'

The change in Kittinger's outlook did not pass unnoticed at Ground Control. The voice now coming through from the stratosphere was neither that of the regular Joe Kittinger nor of the anxiously burbling pilot of a few moments before. Instead, it was focused and stirringly eloquent. Marvin Feldstein felt himself almost moved to tears. As he explained, 'I realised why his remarks produced such a profound response in me: these were the words of a departing man.' Such was Kittinger's dedication to the mission, Feldstein now understood, that he wanted to make sure nothing was left unrecorded. 'He wanted to be certain,' Feldstein wrote, 'that the dangerous beauty he had fought against would not be lost.'

'Everybody's with you, Joe,' he radioed up, with a lump in his throat.

'Always helps to have so many people on the ground praying for me,' Kittinger replied, with feeling. 'With all that help I should make it.'

Chapter Twelve

AT THE TOP

After rising for nineteen and a half vertical miles, *Excelsior* came to a halt at one minute to seven. And as the balloon came to rest, something similar happened inside the soul of its passenger.

During the ascent, Kittinger had been in a continuous state of anxiety about what lay ahead. Now that he knew he would be going no higher, he could finally indulge in a sense of triumph. He had survived this far intact. His pressure suit was still inflated and the helmet had remained on his shoulders. For a few privileged moments, he allowed himself to take in where he was.

The balloon was now drifting westwards, caught in a deliciously stable current of wind. For despite the low atmospheric density, there is indeed wind in the stratosphere, albeit a different animal from the one we know at the surface. Stratospheric wind is extraordinarily thin by terrestrial standards. It is also surprisingly predictable. Initially, it was believed to flow exclusively to the west. In August 1883, Mount Krakatoa in Indonesia erupted, sending volcanic dust high into the atmosphere. Meteorologists, observing that this debris circled the equator in a westerly direction in just thirteen days, concluded that this implied an invariable pattern in the behaviour of air currents several miles above the ground. Eventually, however, a stranger truth emerged. For twenty-six months in succession, the wind in the stratosphere flows to the east. Then it reverses, and moves in the opposite direction for exactly the same length of time. Successive wind regimes first appear at an altitude of more than eighteen miles, then descend at a rate of 0.6 miles per month. The cycle is known as quasi-biennial oscillation, and it is not well understood.

Although *Excelsior* was travelling sideways at 30 m.p.h., she maintained her vertical height of 102,800 feet without the slightest deviation. During her ascent through the troposphere, she had drifted somewhat to the east. Down in the Ground Control hut, Duke Gildenberg calculated that she would be directly over the landing target in eleven minutes. He also kept a careful eye on a small break in the clouds to the west of the target area. If this window should enlarge, Kittinger would be instructed to delay his jump until *Excelsior* was straight above it. This gave him a minimum of 660 seconds at the top. He relayed his impressions to a spellbound ground crew.

'We're at 103,000 feet. Looking out over a very beautiful, beautiful world . . . As you look up the sky looks beautiful but hostile. As you sit here you realise that man will never conquer space. He will learn to live with it but he will never conquer it.

'I can see for over four hundred miles. Beneath me I can see the clouds . . . They are beautiful . . . Looking through my mirror the sky is absolutely black. Void of anything . . . I can see the beautiful blue of the sky and above that it goes into a deep, dark, indescribable blue, which no artist can ever duplicate. It's fantastic.'

For eleven minutes of effortless floating, Kittinger enjoyed the widest-angle view of anyone in history. His was the perspective of a highly privileged angel. Everything around him was utterly silent and still, except for the slowly rotating gondola. From this revolving throne in the heavens, he could see a 780-mile diameter section of the Earth's surface. He was gazing down on almost half a million square miles of sky. Even though he was looking for the most part at land rather than sea, the Earth was washed with blue. Our planet, as viewed from space, appears blue not because the sea is, but because the sky is. From this vantage-point, with the sky literally beneath him, Kittinger could see it for what it really was – a thin shield of illuminated particles that once again obscured the clean line of the Earth's horizon that he had convinced himself he should be seeing.

The cloudscape below was almost infinitely varied in texture, but the patch directly under him resembled a giant, ridged fingerprint. The distinctive large thundercloud that caught his eye to the west was at that moment hanging over Flagstaff, Arizona, 350 miles away. Then he noticed to his astonishment that there were clouds at his level too, ghostly cirrus-like entities that were only visible close to the Sun, but which then reflected its light with a dazzling whiteness. During Man High II, David Simons had observed thin yellowish-brown bands at the point where the sky merged into the blackness of space. He had attributed them to dust thrown up by volcanoes or nuclear explosions, but this description didn't seem to fit what Kittinger was looking at. Perhaps they were noctilucent clouds that for some reason appeared deceptively low in the sky. Their precise identity would remain a mystery.

The Sun brought to mind the Old Testament dictum that 'you cannot face God and live'. Kittinger was partially surrounded by an aluminised anti-glare curtain, but in the rarefied atmosphere of the stratosphere, the blazing was remorseless. Rays of sunlight poured into the gondola through the door and under the curtain like vicious needles. And because most of the blue component of its light had yet to be scattered away by the atmosphere, the great orb no longer looked yellow. Instead, it was white.

Kittinger searched in vain for the stars. He seemed to be in an impossible place. It was dark and there were no clouds overhead, yet the constellations were invisible. In fact, they had been put out by the dazzle. Unshielded by the atmosphere, the Sun burned with the full intensity of its majesty. Yet it seemed curiously isolated, not lighting the sky around it as it did when viewed from the Earth.

There were many other curiosities in this strange new environment. Kittinger was now so far above the Earth that he weighed about three pounds less than he had ninety minutes before, due to a slight reduction in the planet's gravitational pull on him. Atmospheric pressure, which at ground level stood at over one thousand millibars of mercury, was now down to less than nine. The remaining air was charged with radiation, and drier than any bone. Yet amazingly, there was still life at this altitude: the thin, thin soup of microbes and fungi spores known to biologists as aeroplankton.

Kittinger's hand was now like a large block of ice, but amid the wonders of the stratosphere, he scarcely noticed.

———

As spectacular as his vantage-point was, Kittinger was actually less than half a per cent further from the core of the planet than he had been ninety minutes before. Yet he was now in an environment utterly inimical to human life. Such was the fragility of the life-sustaining layer of gases he had left behind. Despite the inhospitable surroundings, the temperature was actually some sixty degrees Fahrenheit (thirty-three degrees Celsius) higher than it had been at the coldest point of the ascent. The reason for this was simple: at this moment, Kittinger was bang in the middle of the celebrated ozone layer.

Our planet is constantly bombarded by waves of electromagnetic radiation, shot into space by the Sun as it burns 93 million miles away from us. These waves come in a range of sizes, which determine their precise characteristics. Most of the radiation that reaches the Earth falls within the visible or infrared part of the spectrum, warming the planet and allowing us to see. About 10 per cent of it, however, has a wavelength shorter than 390 millionths of a millimetre, or nanometres. This is ultraviolet radiation (or UVR), and it has more energy – and therefore more destructive potential – than any other part of the spectrum.

One billion years ago, primitive organisms called blue-green algae began to float in the Earth's primordial oceans. They fed themselves by harnessing electromagnetic radiation from the Sun and using it to break down molecules of water and carbon dioxide. Then they recombined the building blocks of these substances, in particular carbon and hydrogen, to manufacture the organic chemicals they needed to survive. The by product of this process was oxygen, and it began to accumulate in the atmosphere. This was the 'regular' form of the gas, consisting of molecules made up of two joined atoms.

Whenever one of these oxygen molecules was hit by UVR with a wavelength shorter than 240 nanometres, a reaction known as photolysis took place. First, the molecule absorbed the UVR, then it split into two single atoms, or free radicals. If one of these free radicals then ran into a molecule of oxygen before it could find another singleton – a likely occurrence – the two combined. The result was a new, tri-atomic molecule: ozone. Bit by bit, the newly formed molecules of ozone began to cluster together, forming a distinct but vastly diluted layer.

Ozone (O_3) is a miraculous substance. Highly reactive and lethal if inhaled, it is a colourless gas with the smell of burning electrical wiring. Near the ground, it is generated in tiny amounts by lightning bolts and sparking plugs. Even in the stratosphere it is rare, reaching a maximum concentration of only about eight parts per million. If all the ozone in the atmosphere could somehow be collected and brought down to the surface at normal atmospheric pressure, it would form a layer only an eighth of an inch thick. Yet without this irritating, corrosive gas, the Earth would be uninhabitable.

The reason the ozone layer is so important to terrestrial life is that its molecules absorb the most dangerous wavelengths of ultraviolet light long before they ever reach the ground. UVR falls into three ranges. UV-A, with a wavelength of 315–390 nanometres, is the least dangerous. Overexposure can lead to sunburn, but it is deemed safe enough for use in solariums. UV-B (280–315 nm), which can also burn the skin, is much more harmful, and has been implicated in skin cancer and eye damage. Radiation at the shorter end of this range is easily absorbed by proteins, which can interfere with the immune system. But the real villain of the piece is UV-C (100–280 nm). Wavelengths within this band, particularly those around the 260-nanometre mark, are readily absorbed by DNA. If UV-C gets to almost any kind of life form, it will kill it or damage it irreparably.

UVR is still abundant in sunlight when it arrives in the stratosphere. As we saw earlier, the shortest wavelengths are intercepted by ordinary oxygen molecules, via the process of photolysis. But O_2 molecules are powerless when it comes to anything larger than about 240 nanometres. Fortunately, at this point ozone takes up the task, absorbing nearly all the UVR in the 240–320-nanometre range. It lets through all of the UV-A, enabling human beings to cultivate their tans; a little of the UV-B, making it most advisable that they do not overdo it; and none of the UV-C, which allows them to carry on living. There was plenty of UV-C about where Joe Kittinger was.

The ozone layer, then, converts lethal solar energy into harmless heat. In this way, it is like a bulletproof vest for the eco-system. Without the protection of this shield, life would never have survived its first forays on to dry land 600 million years ago. This in itself should give us cause to wonder. But the real miracle of O_3, the reason why it is so effective as a shield, is its extraordinary ability to re-create itself.

The secret of ozone is this. When a molecule of the gas absorbs a beam of UVR, it splits into a regular oxygen molecule and a free radical. But, as we have seen, when a free radical runs into a molecule of O_2, they combine to form another ozone molecule. And O_2 molecules are common in the stratosphere. So every time an ozone molecule sacrifices itself in taking out a dangerous solar missile, another one promptly pops up somewhere else.

In this way, the ozone layer is like Moses' bush in the book of Exodus. It burns, but is never consumed. Religious language seems strangely appropriate in the context of this magical chain-reaction in the sky. In Indian theology, the world owes its existence to the combined action of three godheads: Brahma, the creator, Vishnu, the sustainer, and Shiva the destroyer. High in the stratosphere, life on Earth is sustained by the endless creation and destruction of ozone. Up here, the Shiva and Brahma principles are locked together in an eternal dance.

Or almost eternal. In recent times, concern has arisen that man-made pollutants may be skewing the odds in this cycle of destruction and re-creation. It was in 1974 that Molina and Rowland first suggested that CFCs could alter the balance of this vital and delicate process by reacting with free radicals in the atmosphere. At the time of Excelsior III, however, such anxiety lay in the future. The ozone layer was simply something for Kittinger to wonder at and be grateful for.

———

Although Kittinger was now well above the 'visible' sky, and although 99 per cent of the mass of the atmosphere now lay beneath him, in terms of traversing its total expanse, he knew that he had barely got started. Not for perhaps another six hundred miles would the Earth's gravity finally relinquish its grip on the last few atoms of the atmosphere. Only then would the attenuating mantle of gases surrounding the planet finally blend into the emptiness of interplanetary space. Between that ill-defined boundary and the point where Kittinger now hung suspended, great oceans of upper atmosphere waited to be explored.

Poised on the beach of the ocean of space, he was perfectly placed to ponder the future of the species. 'I looked at space,' he explained later, 'the first man ever to see through only a thin faceplate the environment we were sworn to storm . . .'

If a balloonist was somehow enabled to continue beyond the point at which *Excelsior* had come to a halt, he would find himself passing through a series of distinctive layers. These would seemingly confirm the Ancient Greek hunch that the heavens are arranged concentrically. For the first ten miles or so beyond Kittinger's current location of 100,000 feet, he would feel the temperature continuing to rise, as the warming effect of the ozone layer approached its maximum. At the top of the stratosphere, temperatures of 64°F/18°C have been recorded, equivalent to a pleasant spring day in northern Europe.

About thirty miles above the Earth, the temperature would begin to stabilise, in line with declining concentrations of ozone. Then it would start to fall again with altitude, just as it does in the troposphere. The balloon would now be entering the mesosphere, the most frigid region of all. Here, temperatures fall to −220°F/−140°C, and pressure is down to less than a thousandth of an atmosphere. Yet the remaining gas still provides enough friction to burn up meteors, millions of which fizzle out in the mesosphere every day. As their relics, they leave behind tiny particles of smoke.

Small amounts of the gas methane are constantly making their way to the mesosphere. When they arrive, they are broken down by solar radiation, and water vapour is created as a by-product. This then condenses around nuclei of meteor dust and freezes. The process is thought to be the origin of noctilucent clouds, mysterious streaks of pearly-blue that are occasionally seen in the twilight sky. They are only ever observed shortly after sunset on otherwise cloudless days, illuminated in the mesosphere by the last rays of the dying Sun while the world beneath already lies in darkness.

After twenty miles of travelling through the mesosphere, our hero would notice the temperature starting to rise once again. At the same time, he would find his environment growing increasingly cold. This cryptic remark reflects the fact that there would now be very few particles left, but the ones that remained would be moving around furiously. Heat is a measure of the total kinetic energy in a substance, while temperature only concerns the energy of its average atom. In the thermosphere, the total energy might be paltry, but the average is phenomenal.

The reason particles in the thermosphere tend to be so active is that they are constantly bombarded by photons – 'packages' of electromagnetic energy, of which visible light is a subset, shot in our direction in prodigious numbers by the Sun. The further a particle is from the Earth's surface, the more likely it is to be hit by a high-energy photon, because fewer of these missiles will already have been taken out of the game. More missiles multiplied by fewer targets equals more collisions. As a result, temperatures at the fringe of the thermosphere can rise to a staggering 3630°F/2000°C.

These high-altitude collisions tend to strip atoms of their electrons, converting them into electrically charged ions. Such particles form what is known as a plasma, the so-called fourth state of matter. The ions then form into bands, according to their species/molecular mass. For this reason, the thermosphere is sometimes known as the ionosphere. Radio waves of certain frequencies can be deliberately bounced off these ionised strata. Prior to the advent of satellites, this trick was the key to long-range radio communication. Meanwhile, high above the polar regions, the Earth's magnetic alignment captures ions and electrons sent streaming into space by solar storms, and pulls them down towards the surface. As they unite and separate in the thermosphere, they give off flashes of red and green light. These are the magnificent aurorae.

Far beyond even the thermosphere, the recently discovered Van Allen Belts awaited, obscure bands of protons and electrons thousands of miles outside the atmosphere, which shielded the planet from the fierce solar wind. All of these uncharted regions and more lay ahead for other voyagers. But now, for Joe Kittinger, it was enough to be where he was.

Yet however incomprehensibly magnificent the view from his balcony in the heavens might be, this was not where Kittinger belonged. With a sudden pang, he found himself yearning for the beautiful planet from which he had become separated. Down there was safety and air and all that was familiar. The fall ahead might kill him, but he was starting to look forward to it.

With ninety seconds remaining, Kittinger casually dropped into the conversation that his right hand was not pressurized. Marvin Feldstein almost fell off his chair. He had visions of the entire pressure suit collapsing at any moment. It had been his intention to deliver an inspiring little speech at this juncture, but on hearing this revelation that plan went straight out of the window. The doctor was left itching to know more. But Kittinger had carefully timed his confession to pre-empt the possibility of a long interrogation. 'OK. No sweat. No sweat,' he radioed down, as if to an over-solicitous relative. Feldstein was forced to take his word for it. Seconds later,

Kittinger detached the radio antenna as part of the pre-jump ritual, and all communication with the ground crew was cut off. Now they would have to rely on the radar tracking his falling body and wait in hope for the sudden slowing that would indicate his parachute had opened. For the next five minutes, they would have no way of knowing if Kittinger was alive or dead.

For the first part of his final minute on the edge of space, Kittinger systematically disconnected himself from the life-support system of the gondola. From this point onwards, he would draw his oxygen from an ingenious seat-kit strapped to his backside. This simple red box also contained equipment to record every detail of what was to follow: Kittinger's vital signs, his verbal observations and his rate of fall. It even housed a cine-camera to capture it all on film.

As soon as he began to work, Kittinger realised just how much the ascent had taken out of him. To some extent, the causes of his exhaustion were physical. A measure of fatigue was to be expected in someone who had been wearing 150 pounds of clothing for several hours. But it was the tremendous expenditure of nervous and emotional energy *en route* that had drained him most.

The mere thought of the exertion it would take to get up and shuffle over to the doorway pushed Kittinger's heart-rate up by thirty beats per minute. Nevertheless, he summoned the energy to haul himself up, and edged towards the exit. For forty-five seconds, he stood motionless on the edge of the chasm. Then he gazed up to the highest point in the sky, and shook a defiant mental fist at it. Unwelcome images from Excelsior I raced briefly through his mind, but Kittinger quickly replaced them with more encouraging memories from the second jump. Then he pushed the button that activated the eleven onboard cameras, and prepared to depart. His final task was to pull the lanyard that operated the timer for his stabilisation chute, the process that had proved so troublesome during Excelsior I. With his right hand redundant, this was now beyond him. He would just have to trust the falling weight of his body to provide the necessary yank.

Kittinger took a last, lingering look at the beauties of the stratosphere, and spoke a heartfelt prayer: 'Lord, take care of me now.' Then he stared down at the Earth, laid out beneath him like a swimming-pool, and stepped out into the void.

Chapter Thirteen

THE FALL

The act of leaping from a great height is a highly unnatural one. It requires the overruling of a survival instinct developed over aeons. There is a simple reason for this: if our simian ancestors had been in the habit of throwing themselves off trees, they would never have survived to reproduce. The ones who did were those with a healthy respect for gravity. We have therefore evolved a hardwired aversion to falling, and to situations likely to promote it. From birth to the age of about four months, a startled baby will automatically throw open its arms before quickly drawing them back in again, as if it is trying to clutch at something. This is the Moro reflex, and it is self-evidently designed to minimise the risk of falling. Yet the ability to override such instincts has been at the heart of our success as a species. It has allowed us to conquer the globe, and one day it will allow us to colonise space.

When a person steps from an aeroplane, or leaps from a bridge with a bungee rope tied around their ankles, what usually happens is that they start by falling at a rate familiar to anyone who has ever dived from the high board at the local swimming-baths. If they refrain from opening a parachute, however, they rapidly – and rapidly is the word – accelerate to a speed that the average novice is likely to find highly disturbing. The wind roars ever louder in their ears and the ground seems to rush up to meet them. They will see and feel, in fact, exactly what a person would see and feel in the last few moments before their violent death. At the visceral level, the experiences are identical.

When Kittinger stepped out of the gondola, he went through something rather different. For the first sixteen seconds, he held his breath. During that period, he experienced a silence as profound as any hearing person ever could. On Earth, there would always be a background hum, whether of traffic, planes or wind. But here in the stratosphere, even if there had been anything to make a noise, there was insufficient air around to conduct it. In this and many other curious ways, Kittinger did not seem to be in a 'real' place at all, at least in terms of his familiar frames of reference. Whatever the law of gravity might say, for example, he didn't seem to be falling. There was absolutely no sensation of downward movement. When he changed his bodily attitude, which he was able to do quite easily, it felt like he was rolling over on an invisible flat surface. As he turned, the earth and the sky revolved around him as though he was the centre of the universe. This was at least as weird as anything that Aristotle had imagined.

The thought entered Kittinger's head that perhaps some part of his equipment had snagged on the gondola, hence his apparent suspension in space. It was only when he turned to face upwards that he realised how wrong he was. At first, the balloon, which was now distended to its full diameter of 200 feet, shone painfully white against the blackness of space and filled his field of vision. But within seconds, it had shrunk to the size of a pinprick. In the absence of any other visual cues, Kittinger's brain initially interpreted this to mean that *Excelsior III* was hurtling up into the sky at a fantastic rate. In fact, it was he who was moving, his velocity increasing by 22 m.p.h. every second.

Kittinger's one big disappointment was that once again he was unable to see the stars. He had hoped, once free of the restricting perspective of the gondola, to enjoy a view of the heavens unparalleled in human history. Just him and the vastness of space, with nothing but his faceplate in between. In fact, as he soon recognised, he had been light-blinded by the Sun. Nevertheless, there were plenty of compensations. For sixteen eternal seconds, Kittinger existed in a soundless, motionless world in which he might as well have been pure spirit.

The first reminder of his corporeality was the brief tremor in his back that told him the BMSP was about to spring into action. But though he braced himself in anticipation of a slight opening shock, it never came. For a moment, he wondered whether he shouldn't open the stabilisation 'chute manually. Then he discovered that his left hand, racing ahead of his mind, had already migrated to the D-ring. He soon became aware that he wouldn't need to use it. He was falling feet first. This meant the stabilising drogue 'chute must have opened. Only now could Kittinger let himself breathe. Whatever else might happen, there would be no repeat of Excelsior I.

For the remainder of the fall, Kittinger was to dictate his reactions into the tape-recorder stored in the seat pack beneath him. Under the circumstances, this was a godsend. It was good to have someone to talk to, even if it was only himself. And if something were to go wrong, at least his words had a chance of surviving him. Kittinger's running commentary would provide the scientists with a unique degree of insight into his state of mind during the descent. The transcripted version has a similar effect:

''Chute opened . . . starting to pull.'

Just before making this statement, Kittinger takes his first breath since leaving the gondola. From this point onwards, his eyes will stay glued to the altimeter/stopwatch strapped to his wrist. Only through making periodic reports on his altitude and duration of fall will he be able later to reconstruct the precise context of his utterances.

'Thirty seconds.' He has already fallen almost two and a half miles. At 90,000 feet, his velocity is an astonishing 614 m.p.h. The Earth is pulling her offspring towards her like a magnet.

'Multistage is working perfectly!' Already, the first jump seems a distant memory.

'Can't get my breath. Can't get my . . . breath.' Kittinger is gripped by a sudden terror. Something is pressing down on his windpipe. For fifty seconds he struggles not to black out.

'Stabilised perfect!' The choking sensation vanishes as capriciously as it began. Kittinger flies past the points at which he bailed out of *Excelsiors I* and *II*. Never has he felt so alive. He is jubilant.

'Seventy thousand.' Elation is coursing through Kittinger now. The feeling is like an extended orgasm. He is a tiny sperm rushing to meet its egg.

'Perfect stability.' For the first time, he can feel a slight ripple of air resistance on his pressure suit. The stabilisation 'chute is working so well that he is able to experiment with turning, using his limbs as rudders.

'Beautiful!' The fall is becoming more enjoyable by the second. Kittinger is going home.

'Minute and thirty-five seconds . . .

'Multistage . . . beautiful stability . . . multistage perfect!' He can hardly believe how well the BMSP is functioning.

'Sixty thousand.' No risk now of boiling just through being alive. Kittinger is re-entering the protective blue haze of the sky.

'Fifty thousand.' If his pressure suit were to fail now, he knows he could survive. The thickening atmosphere has slowed him right down to 250 m.p.h. In less than twenty seconds, he will be beneath the critical breathing boundary of 43,000 feet.

'Perfect stability . . .

'I'm going to turn to the right . . . beautiful . . . perfect!'

Kittinger is starting to play now. He moves round to face north, towards the city of Albuquerque.

'Faceplate getting fogged up.' This is the coldest point in the descent. The temperature is −98°F/−72°C. As Kittinger falls, the windblast takes the heat from his face mask so fast that a mist forms around the edges in spite of the integrated heating element.

'Forty thousand.

'Two minutes thirty seconds . . . out of positive pressure.' Blessed release as the pressure suit finally loosens its grip.

'The faceplate fogged up a little bit.

'Thirty-five thousand.' At this point, if an intercontinental jet happened to cruise by, its passengers would see a man hurtling towards them out of the sky.

'Little cold in my legs.' This may be interpreted to mean that they are freezing. Kittinger is not given to hyperbole.

'Thirty thousand . . . No, correction, thirty-four . . .

'Coming up on three minutes. Perfect stability!

'Faceplate's getting fogged up . . . taking off my sun-visor . . . Can't get it loose . . . Here we go, it's off. Maybe that will help. Awful bright . . .' Although Kittinger feels that he is back in familiar territory, he is still well above the peak of Mount Everest. The solar glare is fearsome.

'Thirty thousand.

'Three minutes thirty seconds. Undercast beneath me.' Soon he will be able to breathe without supplemental oxygen.

'Perfect stability!' It all seems so improbable that he has to keep reminding himself.

'Override in my hand for the pack opening.' He is going to take no chances with the main parachute.

'Coming up on twenty thousand! Multistage is beautiful . . . perfect stability . . .

'Four minutes. The undercast beneath me.' The thought is

as yet only at the periphery of Kittinger's consciousness, but he is not looking forward to falling into it.

'The multistage is going perfect . . . beautiful!

'Four minutes ten seconds . . .

'I can turn around perfect. Can do everything!' By now, he is feeling omnipotent.

'Twenty thousand. Four minutes twenty-five seconds . . .

'Four minutes thirty seconds. We're going into the overcast . . .'

Suddenly, he changes the prefix he uses for the cloud-cover. Kittinger has never fallen through clouds before. Intellectually he knows that they are not solid, but can't help bracing himself as the phantom moment of impact approaches. At this point, as the cardiogram will later reveal, his heart-rate increases noticeably.

'Into the overcast!

'The main 'chute just opened, right on the button . . . Four minutes and thirty-seven seconds free-fall!' During this time, Kittinger has dropped more than sixteen miles. This is almost the distance between England and France. The island of Manhattan is only twelve miles from tip to tip. He has demolished the existing free-fall record.

'Eighteen thousand feet . . . aaaaaaaah, boy!'

Now that Kittinger knows he is safe, he finally allows himself to let go. For the next two minutes, as the relief floods through him, he mouths an incredulous prayer of gratitude: 'Thank you, God, thank you . . . thank you for protecting me during that long descent. Thank you, God. Thank you . . .'

He isn't going to die, after all.

Chapter Fourteen

EDEN

As Kittinger emerged from the clouds, he was greeted by twin Chinook helicopters that would circle around him for the remainder of his descent. Emotionally drained as he was, he still had several tasks to perform before landing. Largely on automatic pilot, he disconnected his electric gloves and socks, and disarmed the emergency reserve 'chute. Then he cut loose the left side of the instrument kit strapped beneath him, and swung it on to his lap. In theory, he was supposed to disconnect the six 'hoses' that had linked the pack to the various sensors on his body, then cut away its right side too. At this stage, if all went to plan, it would fall independently until the deployment of a mini-parachute of its own. In the event, with one hand out of action, he managed five of the hoses then gave up. After what he'd been through, it scarcely seemed to matter. He'd just have to land with the pack hanging from one side.

Thirteen minutes and forty-five seconds after stepping from his platform in the sky, Kittinger and his mother planet were reunited. It was a harsh landing, and in the process his leg was severely bruised by the dangling instrument pack. The spot where he landed was a desolate one, objectively speaking, a wilderness of sand, salt grass and sage. The temperature was close to 100°F/38°C. But for Kittinger it was as if he had fallen into the Garden of Eden. Nature herself seemed to conspire in this illusion. While he had been absent, an unseasonable shower had fallen from the same cloudbank that had so plagued his ascent. It was as if the desert was blooming to mimic his emotions.

The two helicopters landed, decanting a stream of medics, colleagues, journalists and friends who rushed towards the prostrate Kittinger. Immediately, they set about removing his helmet and heavy flying gear, handling him like a newborn baby. Kittinger lay back and grinned a lazy grin. 'Gentlemen . . . I'm very glad to be back with you all,' he said. *Life* magazine photographed him bare-chested, smoking a well-earned cigarette.

As Medical Officer Dick Chubb examined his swollen right hand with a mixture of concern and fascination, Kittinger turned to George Post – a particularly interested party as he was scheduled to make the planned fourth Excelsior jump. 'Did you see me hit?' he asked, slightly embarrassed that his descent had ended in such an undignified manner in front of this great parachutist. 'That was no landing. I just came down the best way I could.'

'Joe, I've got news for you,' Post replied. 'Any landing that you walk away from is a good landing.'

At 10 a.m., before he had even had time to call his wife or eat some breakfast, Kittinger was ushered into a briefing room at Holloman to meet the press. Already his right hand was shrinking to its pre-Excelsior dimensions. The journalists were as entranced by his account of the mission as they were by the man himself. They were particularly keen to know what he had been able to see from peak altitude. Kittinger informed them that he had spotted Guadalupe and El Paso in the neighbouring states, but that the Grand Canyon had been obscured by clouds.

The next morning, the full Excelsior team assembled for a debriefing session. They listened enthralled as the tape-recording of Kittinger's descent was played back for the first time. All eyes were on the narrator. At first, Kittinger seemed engrossed in reliving his epic fall. But as the tape wound on to the point where he heard himself thanking God for his deliverance over and over again, a look of puzzled consternation spread across his face. The room was suddenly unbearably tense. 'That is the voice of a coward!' Kittinger blurted out.

It would be difficult to conceive of anyone regarded less as a coward than Joe Kittinger at that moment. Technically what he was saying was rubbish – everyone knew he was an unusually brave man. Nevertheless, the vehemence of his reaction was revealing. The extraordinary truth was that Kittinger had no recollection of his catharsis the previous morning. He felt as though he was listening to someone else. There was more to this amnesia than simple embarrassment at the display of emotional nakedness in an environment where feelings usually went fully clothed. The fact was that Kittinger had repressed the memory. Marvin Feldstein, the project doctor, hypothesised that this was because such displays of emotion were incompatible with Kittinger's self-image. Or perhaps his forgetfulness was a consequence of the sheer intensity of what he had been through: only by erasing his recollection of how the flight ended could he blot out the memory of the terror he had experienced earlier in its course.

This episode served to highlight the inherent difficulty in obtaining an accurate picture of an isolated individual's experiences *in extremis* on the basis of their own subjective reports. The problem was that in the absence of a second opinion, the person in question would have no way of checking the reliability of their memory. The philosopher Wittgenstein had argued that it would be impossible for a man on a desert island to develop a coherent language of his own as he would be unable to tell if he was sticking to its rules. Kittinger's amnesia seemed to provide corroborating evidence.

The next task was to conduct full kit 'hanging' tests for both Joe Kittinger and George Post, to try to pinpoint the cause of the choking Kittinger had experienced during the jump. The chief suspect was a steel cable that attached the back of the helmet to the pressure suit, but the hanging tests were not conclusive. In view of this uncertainty and the demonstrable unreliability of the pressure suit, the fourth jump was cancelled. Post was devastated.

With the project now ended, it was time to reflect on what Excelsior had achieved. First and foremost, Kittinger had proved beyond doubt that it was indeed possible to bail out at super-high altitude and return safely to Earth. Furthermore, he had done it with standard-issue Air Force equipment. Apart from the BMSP, only the heated socks and gloves had fallen outside that category, and they had been there only to protect his extremities during the ascent. The parachute itself had been a triumphant success, as Kittinger's continued existence attested.

There were other lessons to be learned from the earlier portion of the flight. For the first time, it had been shown that a man could expend considerable energy in a space environment without significant untoward effects. Indeed, it was now known that he could even survive a partial failure of his pressure suit. Much had also been learned about the psychological strains to which a lone astronaut might expect to be exposed. This would prove invaluable when it came to selection for future missions.

In the aftermath of Excelsior, Kittinger himself envisaged three ways in which high-altitude balloons could be utilised to further the space effort. In the first place, they could be used for the training of astronauts. However effective laboratory simulations might be, they could never duplicate the spatial separation inherent in space travel. Earthbound subjects would always know that help was close at hand. In a stratospheric balloon, on the other hand, it would be a different story.

A related possibility was the testing of equipment under

the actual conditions under which it was intended to perform. Man High had subjected David Simons' proto space capsule to the only kind of test that could ever be completely convincing. Excelsior had done the same with Kittinger's pressure suit. In future, it would not always be necessary to send people up with the kit under scrutiny. As the entire Excelsior project had been achieved with a cash outlay of some thirty thousand dollars, this proposal was not financially over-ambitious.

A third suggestion was to use high-altitude balloons for astronomical investigation beyond the distorting effects of the atmosphere. Here, Kittinger was far from disinterested: it still rankled with him that he had been unable to see the stars in any of his four journeys to the stratosphere. Two years later, he would be given the opportunity to put this right as the balloon pilot for Project Stargazer, a joint venture between the Navy, Air Force and various academic institutions.

On 13 December 1962, Kittinger and the astronomer William White spent thirteen hours 81,500 feet above Alamogordo, conducting astronomical observations from a fourteen-foot-high, two-ton aluminium gondola. The aims of Stargazer were threefold: to measure high-altitude atmospheric turbulence, to pinpoint the variations it caused in the brightness of stars, and to establish how the light from celestial bodies was affected by airborne water vapour. Unfortunately, the operation was plagued by stabilisation problems. Despite a complex system designed to compensate for the motion of the gondola, the slightest movement of the telescope or its supporting platform turned out to distort an image every bit as effectively as the soupy atmosphere at lower altitudes.

Despite the disappointments of Stargazer I, a second flight was lined up for 20 April 1963. It began and ended farcically. Shortly before the planned take-off, static electricity in the air triggered the release switch designed to separate the gondola from the envelope at the moment of landing. As White and

Kittinger sat nonplussed inside their capsule, the helium-filled envelope shot up into air. And there, with the balloon rushing skywards minus its intended cargo, Joe Kittinger's glorious relationship with the stratosphere came to an end.

Figuratively if not quite literally, Excelsior would turn out to have been the high point in post-war manned high-altitude ballooning. (In May 1961 Malcolm Ross and Victor Prather of the US Navy would reach 113,740 feet in *Strato-Lab V* before, unlike Kittinger, coming down the 'long way'.) As the sixties unfolded, the attention of public and military alike inevitably turned to other, more grandiose missions and to the new selection of heroes who flew them. Less than eight months after Excelsior, Yuri Gagarin became the first man to orbit the Earth. It would not be long before others would escape her gravitational pull altogether. Yet for all their unquestioned courage, it is doubtful whether Gagarin or any of the Mercury, Gemini and Apollo astronauts who followed him could match Joe Kittinger's achievement for sheer guts.

In practical terms, the legacy of Excelsior was disappointing. The Air Force never did adopt the BMSP, preferring instead to encourage high-altitude pilots in trouble to refrain from ejecting until they reached the lower atmosphere. NASA, too, showed little interest in the Excelsior escape system. Many who had been involved in the project felt that this was essentially a matter of vanity: the Agency, they grumbled, was just too proud to allow itself to be intellectually beholden to anyone else. On 28 January 1986, the sceptics were to be tragically vindicated. Seventy-three seconds after its launch, the *Challenger* Space Shuttle exploded in front of a television audience of millions. At the time, it was at an altitude of 46,000 feet. Kittinger believes that the seven astronauts who died that day were still alive when they hit the water, a possibility that even NASA eventually conceded. If they had been equipped with Beaupre's parachute, they might have survived.

Kittinger himself forsook the opportunity to get involved in the American space programme in favour of serving in Vietnam. Duke Gildenberg believes that, like many pilots of his generation, he would never have been able to convince himself that he was the genuine article until he'd experienced combat first hand. He was also deeply patriotic. In March 1972 he was shot down over North Vietnam. During the eleven months he subsequently spent incarcerated in the infamous 'Hanoi Hilton', Kittinger, like Jacques Garnerin under similar circumstances during the 1790s, had plenty of time to plan his next great project: the first solo crossing of the Atlantic in a balloon. Once again, his determination found a way. In 1984, Kittinger emerged from the gondola of the *Rosie O'Grady* in Savona, northern Italy, having negotiated a 3,543-mile journey from Maine. Yet another record was in the bag.

Joe Kittinger is still flying. He is an expert skywriter, making something of a speciality of the smiley face. He remains philosophical about the fact that, from a purely pragmatic perspective, Excelsior failed to lead anywhere much. After all, as he himself maintains, 'If life is not an adventure, then it is nothing at all.'

After the early 1960s, no government would again send a human being to the stratosphere at one end of a glorified plastic bag. The technology on which Man High and Excelsior had depended was to be dramatically superseded during the following decade, and the projects themselves were rapidly forgotten in the excitement of the race for the Moon. But a line had been crossed that could never be erased. People had broken through the skin of the sky and seen with their own eyes what lay on the other side. Through Project Excelsior, man had achieved his oldest dream. And he had done it for less than thirty thousand dollars.

EPILOGUE

The Pueblo Indians of New Mexico live in a beautiful but stark environment. Theirs is an ancient land, dotted with mesas, the eroded skeletons of mountains. The earth is very red, the clouds are very white and the sky is very blue. And the Sun, in the clear, high desert air, somehow seems more dominant than anywhere else.

All native peoples are interested in the sky, but the Pueblos are unusual in paying more attention to its daytime manifestation than its appearance by night. There are good reasons for this. Life here is lived on the margin. Agricultural activity must be precisely co-ordinated with the seasons, and the Sun, given careful observation of the points at which it rises and sets on the horizon, provides a far more accurate calendar than the Moon.

There is also another consideration. In this arid part of the world, the most precious commodity is water. Accordingly, much Pueblo ritual is concerned with the generation of clouds. In less censorious times, 'cloud blowers' or tobacco pipes were smoked to stimulate rain. The underlying principle here – that like produces like – also explains the prevalence of lightning and raincloud motifs in the exquisite pottery for which the Pueblos are famous. Clouds are sometimes thought of as the breath of the dead.

Among archaeologists, the conventional explanation for the presence of Native Americans in the continent is a migration of their ancestors across the Bering Straits about fourteen thousand years ago. The Pueblo Indians have a rival theory.

They believe that 'the People' emerged from the Earth itself. In some villages, they will even point your way to the *sipapu*, the local version of this entrypoint. A symbolic mini-*sipapu* is dug into the floor of every *kiva*, the round edifice that lies at the heart of Pueblo ceremony.

Most tribes believe that man had to travel through not just one but a series of worlds before he emerged into his present environment. The usual number is four. The inhabitants of Zuni Pueblo paint a bleak picture of the first world. It was filled with 'unfinished creatures, crawling like reptiles one over another in filth and black darkness, crowding thickly together and treading on each other, one spitting on another or doing some other indecency'. There was therefore plenty of incentive to move onwards and upwards.

The way was paved by a kind of messiah figure, Póshai-yank'ya, who made his way to the surface of our current world via routes too complex for the others to follow. There he besought the Sun to liberate mankind and the other creatures from their imprisonment below. The Sun's response was to bring into being a pair of divine twins, who descended into the underworld to lead the people up to the surface.

When the Twins arrived in the lowermost world, they found vine-like plants growing in the darkness. When they breathed on the stems, they began to grow miraculously, climbing upwards towards a chink of light visible through the cleft in the ceiling of the first world. This had been made by the bolt of lightning used by the Twins to blast a way for their downward journey.

Up this Jack-and-the-Beanstalk ladder the people climbed, closely followed by the Twins. The second world was somewhat roomier than the first, but still far from satisfactory. So the Twins breathed on the vines again, and the proto-humans and animals passed through another sky into world number three. The people ascended in six waves, the members of each becoming the ancestors of a different race.

Light conditions in the third world were somewhat improved, with visibility comparable to that provided by starlight. But eventually this level also became overpopulated, and the inhabitants were led upwards once more. As with each preceding transition, not all of them made it.

Even in the penultimate world, which glowed like a red dawn, the people were far from complete, with webbed feet and 'no mouths or exits'. Nevertheless, many believed that they had arrived at their final destination. To their dismay, however, the Twins informed them that there was still one more leg of the journey to go. But eventually, after four ages underground, the people finally emerged into the wondrous light of the surface:

When they came into the sunlight, the tears ran down their cheeks. Younger brother [of the Twins] said to them, 'Turn to the Sun and look full at our father the Sun, no matter how bright it is.' They cried out, for it hurt them, and their tears ran to the ground. Everywhere they were standing, the Sun's flowers sprang up from the tears caused by the Sun. The people said, 'Is this the world where we shall live?'

'Yes, this is the last world. Here, you see our father Sun.'

But perhaps the Zunis are wrong. Maybe this is not the final world after all. Maybe, one day, the human race will move on once again.

The Man High and Excelsior projects were the culmination of a logic that has been unfolding since prehistoric times. The vertical imperative, it seems, is written into our very being. Humans have always sought to expand into new territory, and from the moment men first left the ground, it was inevitable that this drive would ultimately lead them to the threshold of space.

The individuals who took us there deserve to be more than just footnotes to history. One day, our descendants may argue that there have been two quantum leaps in evolution: first, the migration of life-forms from the sea on to the dry land about 450 million years ago; second, the departure of men from the greater ocean of the atmosphere in the 1950s and 1960s, fuelled by little more than willpower.

In the meantime, the achievements of the high-altitude balloonists should stand proudly in the sky as monuments to the human spirit. Already, the vistas enjoyed by Kittinger, Simons and the astronauts who came after them have had a transformative effect on our consciousness. Images of Earth from space have shown us our interconnectedness and the miraculous fragility of the thin band of gases in which we live more effectively than any rhetoric ever could. But the very fact that we have access to this viewpoint gives us a glimpse of a possibility we can barely allow ourselves to admit: that one day, our species may find itself saying goodbye to the planet for good.

Perhaps this world, like the early worlds of the Zuni, will become unbearably crowded. Maybe it will just get too hot and dry. Or maybe, right at the point when we are poised to depart, we, like Kittinger, will come to see our Earth as an Eden, as a place it is our duty to nourish and maintain. Whatever happens, we have the comforting knowledge that we already know how to get to the sixth world and back. Men like Joe Kittinger have paved the way on our behalf. They have found the *sipapu*, and punched for us a hole in the sky.

BIBLIOGRAPHY

BOOKS

Anon., *The Air Balloon, or a Treatise on The Aerostatic Globe, Lately Invented by the Celebrated M. Montgolfier of Paris*, G. Kearsley, 1783

Aristotle, *On the Heavens*, trs. W.K.C. Guthrie, Heinemann, 1986

Bacon, John M., *The Dominion of the Air: The Story of Aerial Navigation*, Cassell, 1902

Bates, Jim, *Parachuting: from Student to Skydiver*, Tab Books, 1990

Benedict, Ruth, *Zuni Mythology* (2 vols), Columbia University Press, 1935

Blacker, Carmen, and Loewe, Michaels (eds), *Ancient Cosmologies*, Allen & Unwin, 1975

Carey, John (ed.), *The Faber Book of Science*, Faber & Faber, 1995

Cavallo, Tiberius, *The History and Practice of Aerostation*, C. Dilly, London, 1785

Charles Vivian, E., *A History of Aeronautics*, Collins, 1921

Claxton, William J., *The Mastery of the Air*, Blackie, 1914

Coxwell, Henry, *My Life and Balloon Experiences*, W.H. Allen, 1889

Crouch, Tom D., *The Eagle Aloft: Two Centuries of the Balloon in America*, Smithsonian Institution Press, 1983

DeVorkin, David, *Race to the Stratosphere: Manned Scientific Ballooning in America*, Springer-Verlag, 1989

Doran, Robert, *The Lives of St Simeon Stylites*, Cistercian Publications, 1992

Gillespie, Charles Coulston, *The Montgolfier Brothers and the Invention of Aviation 1783–4*, Princeton University Press, 1983

Glaisher, James, Flammarion, C., De Fonvielle, W., and Tissandier, G., *Travels in the Air*, trs. T.L. Phipson, London, 1871

Haining, Peter, (ed.), *The Dream Machines*, New English Library, 1972

Harper, Harry, *The Evolution of the Flying Machine*, Hutchinson, 1930

Hart, C., *The Dream of Flight: Aeronautics from Classical Times to the Renaissance*, Faber & Faber, 1972

Hearn, Peter, *The Sky People: a History of Parachuting*, Air Life Publishing, 1977

Henry, John, *Moving Heaven and Earth: Copernicus and the Solar System*, Icon Books, 2001

Honour, Alan E., *Ten Miles High, Two Miles Deep: The Adventures of the Piccards*, Brockhampton Press, 1959

Jennings, Peter, and Brewster, Todd, *The Century*, Doubleday, 1998

Kirschner, Edwin J., *Aerospace Balloons from Mongolfier to Space*, Aero, 1985

Kittinger, Captain, Joseph W. Jr, with Caidin, Martin, *The Long, Lonely Leap*, E. P. Dutton, 1961

Lavery, David, *Late for the Sky: the Mentality of the Space Age*, Southern Illinois University Press, 1992

Marion, Fulgence, *Wonderful Balloon Ascents, or the Conquest of the Skies*, London, 1870

McNabb, David, and Younger, J., *The Planets*, BBC Worldwide, 1999

Piccard, Auguste, *Between Earth and Sky*, trs. Apcher, Claude, Falcon Press, 1950

Ray, Benjamin C., *African Religions: Symbol, Ritual and Community*, Prentice-Hall, 1976

Rolt, L. T. C., *The Aeronauts*, Longman, 1966

Ryan, Craig, *The Pre-Astronauts*, Naval Institute Press, 1995

Salzberg, Hugh W., *From Caveman to Chemist*, American Chemical Society, 1991

Simons, Lt Col., David G., with Schanke, Don A., *Man High*, Doubleday, 1960

Strutt, Robert, *Life of Lord Rayleigh*, Edward Arnold, 1924

Swenson, Loyd S., Grimwood, J.M., and Alexander, C.C., *This New Ocean: a History of Project Mercury*, NASA, 1966

Tyler, Hamilton A., *Pueblo Gods and Myths*, University of Oklahoma Press, 1964

Valentine, E. Seton, and Tomlinson, F.L., *Travels in Space: a History of Aerial Navigation*, Hurst & Blackett, 1902

White, Frank, *The Overview Effect*, Houghton Mifflin, 1987

Williams, Henry Smith, *A History of Science*, vol. 4, Harper & Bros, 1904

Wolfe, Tom, *The Right Stuff*, Cape, 1979

ARTICLES

Corfidi, S.F., 'The Colors of Twilight and Sunset', in *Weatherwise Magazine*, June/July 1996

Green, Matthew, 'The Sacred Sky of the Navajo and Pueblo', in *Griffith Observer*, March 1996

Kittinger Jr, Captain Joseph W., 'The Long, Lonely Leap', in *National Geographic*, December 1960

'Space Race Soars With a Vengeance', in *Life*, 29 August 1960

McKenna, Master Sergeant Pat, 'Leap of Faith', in *Airman*, December 1999

Mewaldt, R.A., 'Cosmic Rays', in *Macmillan Encyclopedia of Physics*, London, 1996

'World's Largest Free Balloon to Explore Stratosphere', in *National Geographic*, July 1934

Seely, Paul, 'The Firmament and the Water', in *Westminster Theological Journal*, Fall 1991, Spring 1992, nos 53 and 54

Stevens, Captain Albert W., 'Exploring the Stratosphere', *National Geographic*, October 1934

Stevens, Captain Albert W., 'Man's Farthest Aloft' in *National Geographic*, January 1936

Thomas, David E., 'Obituary of Col. John Paul Stapp', *Skeptical Inquirer*, March 2000

WEB ARTICLES

Cox, Douglas, 'Report on the Firmament', 1996, www.sentex.net/~tcc.firma2.html

Fisher, Gordon, 'Marriage and Divorce of Astronomy and Astrology: A History of Astral Prediction from Antiquity to Newton', 2000, www.gfisher.org

Landis, Geoffrey A., 'Human Exposure to Vacuum', viewed November 2001, www.sff.net/people/geoffrey.landis/vacuum.html

Launius, Roger D., 'Sputnik and the Origins of the Space Age', viewed June 2001, www.hq.nasa.gov/office/pao/History/sputnik/sputorig.html

NASA History Office, 'History of Research in Space Biology and Biodynamics at Holloman Air Force Base 1946–58', updated August 1998, www.hq.nasa.gov/office/pao/History/afspbio/top.htm

'Nazca', viewed October 2001, www.nott.com/nazca.htm

Articles on creation myths, viewed January 2001, www.mythinglinks.org

'Atmospheric Structure' and 'Understanding Ozone', http://daac.gsfc.nasa.gov/CAMPAIGN_DOCS/ATM_CHEM/ozone_atmosphere.html

'Hypoxia: An Analysis of our evolving understanding and management of the phenomenon', http://members.ozemail.com.au/~dxw/Articles/XOHP_121-2.html

'The History of Aviation and Modern Rocketry', viewed August 2001, www.thespaceplace.com/history/rocket2.html

'Man's Escape from Aircraft from the Parachute to a Zero-Zero Escape System' by Andrew R. Jessen, 1966, www.ejectionseat.com/parachut.html

'Going High: The Early Pioneers', updated November 2000, www.pbs.org/wgbh/nova/everest/history/highpioneers.html

'The Zenith Tragedy', viewed June 2001, http://members.tripod.co.uk/vigilant/balloons/zenith.html

Graham, John F., 'Space Exploration from Talisman of the Past to Gateway for the Future', 1995, www.space.edu/projects/book

INDEX